SMART
TRADING PLANS

SMART
TRADING PLANS

**A step-by-step guide to developing
a business plan for trading the markets**

JUSTINE POLLARD

Wrightbooks

First published 2008 by Wrightbooks
an imprint of John Wiley & Sons Australia, Ltd
42 McDougall Street, Milton Qld 4064
Office also in Melbourne

Typeset in Berkeley LT 11.5/14.5pt

© Justine Pollard 2008
<www.smarttrading.com.au>

The moral rights of the author have been asserted

National Library of Australia Cataloguing-in-Publication data:

Author:	Pollard, Justine.
Title:	Smart trading plans / Justine Pollard.
Publisher:	Richmond, Vic. : John Wiley & Sons, 2008.
ISBN:	9780731407866 (pbk.)
Notes:	Includes index.
Subjects:	Speculation. Stock exchanges.
Dewey Number:	332.645

Cover image © iStockphoto/Andrey Volodin

Charts and screenshots © MetaStock

10 9 8 7 6 5 4

Disclaimer

Contents

Acknowledgements

I would like to thank all the people who helped, supported and encouraged me to take on this project and write *Smart Trading Plans*.

First and foremost, my husband Greg, for always believing in me, supporting me and encouraging me to follow my dreams and to write this book, even after the birth of our baby son, who arrived in the early stages of drafting this book.

My mum, Robyn, for always being there for me and helping out with our two beautiful children while I wrote this book. I know you love every minute with the children, but it gave me extra time to focus my energies on writing.

The supportive team at John Wiley & Sons who offered me the opportunity to write *Smart Trading Plans* and assisted me every step of the way.

The mentors I have met along my journey who have made me the trader that I am today.

Finally, to all my clients and readers out there, you are the reason I wrote this book. I know what it is like in those early days of your trading journey, and my goal is to assist you in taking the right steps to get started.

Foreword

I first heard about Justine through my adoptive father, who attended one of her technical analysis classes on Sydney's North Shore several years ago. I was interested in meeting Justine and wanted to find out more about her and her trading. But it was not until 2006, when I was searching for traders to interview for my first book (*Real Traders*), that I finally had an opportunity to meet Justine. I contacted her when I learnt that she had experience in trading contracts for difference (CFDs), and was delighted when she agreed to be featured in my book on the subject.

One of the things that stood out for me after my first meeting with Justine was the fact that she's so thorough and meticulous. I must admit I was not expecting her to show me all the spreadsheets, charts, indicators, templates and trading tools that she had developed herself over the years. I didn't tell her then, but of the many traders I've met and interviewed she's the only one who readily and openly shared the details of her trading methodology.

Since that first interview, Justine and I have developed a close relationship at various levels—I regularly call her to exchange trading ideas, and at times I ask her for media commentaries. Sometimes I consult her on specific trading strategies and pick her brain on various trading situations. In a way, we share a virtual mentoring/ sharing arrangement, which I believe is vital in every trader's journey in dealing with the markets.

Over the years Justine has mentored hundreds, maybe even thousands, of traders and would-be traders. I believe those traders have benefited greatly from Justine's experience, generosity and willingness to help others become successful in the markets.

Just like in her mentoring and coaching programs, Justine tells it how it is in *Smart Trading Plans*. You really have to appreciate the fact that everything she's written is drawn from her years of experience in dealing with the markets. She doesn't try to make trading look easy—instead, she openly and honestly admits that trading is tough. It takes courage and discipline, especially during the hard times, to ensure that you stick to your trading plan. To receive this advice from someone with years of experience who is actively and profitably trading the markets is very valuable.

Justine says that she can give you all the necessary tools and information about the market and trading strategies, but in the end whether you become a successful trader or not will depend on you alone. You will need discipline and determination to succeed, and this book on getting your smart trading plan together will set you on the right path.

This book is not just about making money—it is a blueprint for ongoing wealth creation and a guide to help you focus on your goals and overall lifestyle plans.

Don't let the title of this book deceive you—it is about more than coming up with a smart trading plan. Justine shares many of her personal trading tools, trading routines, techniques, market evaluation processes and analysis methodologies. Again, what makes this stand out from other books is that you can be sure that Justine is sharing everything based on her trading experience. She's not afraid to admit that not all her trades are winners. She openly shares her performance results over the years, and most recently from a CFD trading competition where she managed to generate a return of 82.5 per cent over an eight-week period.

One of the outstanding quotes I remember Justine giving me in an interview was about stop losses. She said, 'Stop losses are my lifeline in the market'. This demonstrates how important risk management is for Justine, and it is no wonder that she dedicates three chapters in this book to emphasising the importance of risk management in your trading.

This must be one of the most inspiring and challenging books on trading and understanding the markets. As Justine said, trading is psychological, and I'm sure you will also come to a better understanding and appreciation of yourself once you've read this book.

For those who want to get started in trading but are not quite certain where and how to begin, this book will give you all the basic and important guidelines you will need to make the best possible start. For those of you who have been trading the market for a while but are still trying to figure it out, this book can help you unlearn some of the bad habits you've picked up along the way. It will also come in handy in reviewing and re-evaluating your trading plan and strategy. And to those who have been in the market for so long that they think there's nothing else to learn, you may be surprised at the wealth of wisdom and knowledge you will find in this book.

Wherever you are in your trading journey, this book will definitely give you a smart push to bring your trading to a higher level.

Eva Diaz

Author,

Real Traders, Real Lives, Real Money

Introduction

A trading plan is your road map in the market—without it you will get lost

When I first began trading the markets for a living, it was nothing like I'd anticipated. I remember dollar signs flashing in front of my eyes—I expected to make large profits and thought it would be easy. I was attracted to short-term trading, thinking the faster and more regularly I traded, the more money I would make. Boy, was I wrong. The reality was very different. It was the most challenging career decision I have ever made and one that was full of self-discovery, discipline, confrontation and going beyond what felt right. In the end, it was also one of my best career choices once I discovered the secrets to trading success—which is all about having a sound trading plan and adhering to strict money management rules.

When publishers from John Wiley & Sons approached me to write this book, I was very excited. As a true believer in the importance of a trading plan, I teach a course called *Smart Trading Plan & System Development*, which revolves around the development of your own personal trading plan. I knew that writing this book felt right, and through it I would be able to get my message about the importance of a trading plan out to more people. Most importantly, this book will teach readers what I believe should go into a trading plan. It's one thing to realise that you need to have a trading plan, but another to know where to start and what to put into it.

I have a background in business and marketing and have been involved in the development of business plans. This knowledge and experience assisted me in developing my own personal trading plan. I styled it on a business plan and adapted it to suit the business of trading.

I then converted my trading plan into a template that I have provided to my clients for many years to assist them in completing and developing their own personal plans. As a special bonus for purchasing this book, I am making this *Smart Trading Plan Template* available to you to download for free. The template is a Microsoft Word document, ready for you to download and work through as you read this book.

To download the template, please visit <www.smarttrading.com.au> and click on 'free book bonuses'. There is also a free *Position Sizing Calculator* available for download, discussed further in chapter 14.

Who am I?

You may already be familiar with me from my interview in the book *Real Traders, Real Lives, Real Money*. Eva Diaz interviewed me for this extraordinary book, based on the lives and experiences of some of Australia's most successful and profitable CFD and FX traders.

I'm a private Australian stock market trader, trading mentor and author of a range of training courses and programs. I not only trade the markets, but enjoy educating budding traders in getting started and improving their skills and knowledge of the markets. You can find out more information about me by visiting my website <www.smarttrading.com.au>.

I was introduced to the stock market by my grandfather after I left high school in the early 1990s. It was not until the end of 2000 that I made the decision to leave my full-time job and trade the stock market for a living. I can't say that my first year of full-time trading was very successful. I traded a lot of different instruments, tried a lot of different styles and experienced the crash in the markets after the events of 11 September 2001. So I know that learning to master trading can be very challenging. It's a topic that is full of overwhelming information and it is always hard to know where to start.

I use technical analysis to make all my trading decisions and I cover this topic in chapter 3. I taught myself how to trade over many, many years and have spent vast amounts of money on my trading education (some of it well spent and some not). It took some time before I finally found the mentors whose styles appealed to me. I then went about developing a style that suited me and continually refined it until it was both simple and mechanical.

I like the mechanical approach to trading and use two systems—a medium-term daily system and a long-term weekly system. My approach is very simple and is all based around trading trends and using strict money management rules to follow the golden rule of trading, which is to let your profits run and cut your losses short. I provide more information on my trading systems in chapter 24 and describe some of my trades from the CMC Markets trading competition in which I achieved an 82.5 per cent return in eight weeks.

I use a charting program called MetaStock and make use of a mechanical filter to scan for entries and a trailing stop-loss indicator for exits. I also incorporate a range of money management techniques to size my trades, manage my maximum open-market risk and boost my winning positions through pyramiding. Charting software, risk management and trading instruments are covered later in this book.

I mostly trade the Australian market through shares and contracts for difference (CFDs) and from time to time I trade the US markets when the opportunities present themselves.

Who is this book for?

If you want to trade like a professional, your first step is to take the time to develop your own personal trading plan.

I have written this book for all traders, whether they are just starting out and looking for a place to begin, or have already been trading and want to set some clear foundations in place by developing a trading plan. Others may want to refine their trading plans to ensure they have covered everything. No matter where you are with your trading, you need to have a plan. Every successful trader has a trading plan—that is what makes them successful and distinguishes them from the amateurs in the markets. If your goal is to be a successful trader (which I know it is because you are reading this book), then you must have a trading plan.

Completing a trading plan is a big task. It's easy to put it off and say you'll do it later, but it is a lot of information to carry around in your head. By taking this information out of your head and writing it down, you are giving your trading perspective, focus and clear guidelines. Plus, you are relieving your mind of the stress of trying to retain all that information and allowing more knowledge to come in. It is well worth the effort and you will feel much more at ease as you move forward with your trading.

About this book

There may be some terms that I use throughout this book that you do not understand. I explain most of these terms as they come up, but to assist you further, I have provided a glossary at the end of the book so that you can look up any terms I mention that you are unfamiliar with.

This book provides you with all the foundations required to complete your own personal trading plan. I can't stress enough the importance of taking the time to do this and that is why I am offering you my *Smart Trading Plan Template* as a special bonus to assist you in doing so.

In order to get the most out of this book, I suggest that you work on a section of this template as you complete each chapter of the book. It will make it a lot easier to complete and it won't feel like such a big task later. You may decide to read the entire book first and then go back and focus on completing your trading plan by re-reading one chapter at a time. Be aware that (at first) your trading plan will be a work in progress and you will continue to refine it as your knowledge grows.

This book covers all the sections that you need to include in your trading plan. From part II onwards, each chapter is dedicated to a specific section. The sections that need to be covered in your plan are:

- goals and objectives

- trading structure

- trading tools

- trading style

- trading indicators

- risk and money management

- market exposure guidelines

- trading systems (including your set-up and trigger criteria for each system and exits)

- trading routine

- trading performance and analysis

- contingency plan for all worst-case scenarios
- personal trading rules.

Within these sections there are a range of subheadings that you will need to cover. For example, the first section of your plan will look something like this:

Goals and objectives

Why am I trading?

Goals

Trading edge

Trading returns and objectives

I discuss each of these subheadings and assist you in completing them. Throughout the book I put forward a series of questions for you to think about that will help you to complete that subsection. I also provide information to guide you in making important decisions, such as selecting your trading style.

As I discuss certain elements, I provide examples of what a long-term trader may put into each subsection of the trading plan. These examples are a guide only and are collated in appendix A at the end of the book to show you how a sample trading plan may look on completion.

Each chapter ends with a 'smart action step' that will guide you in what you need to do to complete that section of your trading plan.

I am looking forward to assisting you in becoming a SMARTER trader and guiding you in completing your own personal trading plan.

Justine

Justine Pollard
Private trader and mentor
<www.smarttrading.com.au>

Part I ▲▲▲ Your business of trading

1

Trading is a business

The oft-quoted statistic is that 80 per cent of traders fail to make money in the markets. One of the reasons such a high percentage fail is because many traders do not have a plan—they trade the markets blindly with no focus and no clear guidelines. Trading is a business and in order for a business to survive, it must have a plan.

When you trade the markets, you are putting money at risk with the goal of achieving a profit, just like any small business. So you need to treat it like a business and have a plan that sets out how you are going to manage it. In essence, this is what this book is all about. It's about teaching you to be a sound businessperson and the steps you need to take to develop your own personal trading plan.

A trading plan is very personal and individual. We are all different and what may suit one trader will not necessarily suit another. As a trader, you are totally responsible for your own decisions and actions in the market, so your plan needs to be unique. It needs to reflect your personal motivations for trading and be based on a method that suits your personality and lifestyle. This will be influenced by how much time you have to devote to trading and the amount of available capital you have to trade.

Develop a SMART trading plan

The only way you can be successful in the markets is to develop a trading plan that suits your personality. It is up to you to lay the foundations yourself and develop your plan to blend with your lifestyle and personality.

My goal is to guide you in developing your own personal SMART trading plan. When I say SMART, I mean that your plan must reflect the following key criteria. I will be covering these in more detail throughout the book.

Simple. Keep your plan simple—it is easy to get bogged down with too much information in trading and overcomplicate it with too many rules. I like the KISS method—'Keep It Simple Stupid'. For a technical trader, it should simply be about trading in the direction of the trend and exiting when the trend changes. But that is always easier said than done, because emotions often come into play and affect your trading decisions.

Mindset. You are the most important part of your trading. It is what goes on inside your head that will make or break you as a trader. You need to develop self-awareness and understand your motives for trading. Trading is not just about making money—money will flow from good trading.

Approach that suits your personality. Trading is about developing an approach that you are comfortable with that suits your personality and lifestyle. Your own personality influences the way you trade. Each person has a different psychological makeup and different reasons for wanting to trade the markets. If your approach does not reflect these things, it is unlikely that you will follow it.

Risk and money management. Managing your risk and money will be one of the keys to your success in the markets. You need to include information in your plan on how you will determine your position size, your capital allocation and stop-loss methods.

Trading system. This is the method you are going to use to trade. Your system will include the signals you will use to enter a trade, such as the set-up and trigger criteria and, most importantly, your exits.

How much capital do you need to get started?

I am often asked, 'What is the minimum equity you need to trade?' Obviously, the more money you have available, the better. But at the same time, you have to start somewhere and learn, even if it is a small amount. It's best to start small first and see if you like trading before committing more money to it. A good starting point would be $10 000 to $20 000. With $10 000, you could take on four trades at $2500 each. Any amount lower than this would make the positions smaller and the brokerage costs proportionally larger. If you have a $20000 account, you could take four trades at $5000 each, or five trades at $4000 each.

You need enough money to allow you to diversify in the market with at least four to five trades and ensure that brokerage costs don't weigh on your account. Because trading is not a zero-sum game, the brokerage costs really add up on small accounts. The cheapest brokerage for share trading is a fixed cost of approximately $19.95 per trade for trades under $10000. So to buy and sell, you are looking at a total of about $40 per trade. At $40 a trade, this would equate to 1.6 per cent of a $2500 trade. So you would require a share to rise by 1.6 per cent just to pay off the brokerage costs of the trade. The smaller the amount invested, the larger the rise you would require to pay for brokerage. This makes it harder to make a profit.

The next question I am often asked is, 'Can I replace my income by trading?' Once again, this depends on your capital base. You have to think of trading in percentage returns. If you are confident that you can make a 20 per cent return on your capital, then you need to consider how much capital you would need to replace your income. For example, 20 per cent return on a $100000 account would provide an income of $20000 — would this be enough to replace your income? Probably not. But it gives you something to think about — you must be realistic about the return you can expect. I will be talking more about trading returns and objectives in chapter 4.

✔ Smart action step

Be a sound businessperson. Make it your goal today to develop your own personal SMART trading plan. To get started, visit <www.smarttrading.com.au> to download your free *Smart Trading Plan Template* and focus on completing it as you read through this book.

2

Trading psychology

All of the top traders I have met and read about say that psychology is the key to successful trading. I did not understand this until I started trading the markets full-time and had to come to terms with the emotional swings and internal dialogue you experience while in a trade. It took me some time to realise how important your mindset is in becoming a successful trader — in the end, this is what makes or breaks you in the markets.

I have learned more about myself since trading the markets full-time than in any other career I have undertaken. I can say now that it has been a wonderful journey of self-discovery and inner growth, but during the first year it definitely did not feel that way. I would like to share with you the psychological journey that I went through in my first year of full-time trading and the steps that I undertook in the following year to improve myself.

My trading journey

Before I started trading the markets full-time, I sat down and studied my motivations, set goals and determined what I thought to be my edge in the market. I knew that I was a highly organised, determined, motivated and goal-oriented person, so I felt that these characteristics would give me an edge in the market. However, I lacked patience and had a tendency to beat myself up after exiting a losing trade.

Patience was elusive. I was always afraid of missing opportunities and the need to be in the market was very overpowering. I found myself attracted to options trading. Everything seemed to happen very fast with options—in only a day or two you knew that your trade was a winner or a loser. The only problem was, I did very well in my first few months of options trading and started to focus on money rather than on good trading. This actually caused me to overtrade, which is not a very successful activity in the market. These are some of the issues I had to learn to deal with as part of my psychological development as a trader.

Once I realised that I was sabotaging myself in the markets, I knew that I had to take action to overcome my problems in order to move to the next level and become a peak performer in the markets. Below are the steps I undertook to get back on track and become the successful trader that I am today.

1. Get to know yourself

Continually work on improving your mindset. You are the most important factor in your trading. You are the one who makes the decisions and you are the one who decides what happens once you open a trade. It is what goes on inside your head that will make or break you as a trader. You need to develop self-awareness and understand your motives for trading. Trading is not just about making money—it's about becoming the best trader you can possibly be.

Start a trading diary. Have a good look at yourself and your personality drivers. Understand how your personality influences the way you trade. Realise your strengths and weaknesses in the market and explore ways of overcoming your weaknesses. I recommend that you start a trading diary and write down your trading emotions each day as they occur and you recognise them. Writing down your thoughts and bad habits as they develop is like sitting back and watching yourself in a mirror. Once you have developed a list, look at the traits you have identified and determine how they might benefit or limit your trading. Think about how you might overcome your limitations.

Source books on self-development. There are a lot of helpful books available on self-development, self-healing and the psychology of trading. One book that I highly recommend is *Trading in the Zone* by Mark Douglas. The subtitle of this book sums up its premise: 'Master the market with confidence, discipline and a winning attitude'.

2. Believe in yourself

Create positive visualisations and a positive internal dialogue. As part of getting to know yourself, you will start to become aware of the things you say silently inside your head. I know that I used to beat myself up after exiting a losing trade. I consistently put myself down and agonised over what could have been. Even though I understood that losing was part of the game of trading and that I must learn from my experiences, it still did not stop me from talking to myself in this way.

To overcome this, I took some courses in self-development and improving my mindset, touching on the basics of NLP (neuro linguistic programming). This helped me to put my life into perspective, gain control over my emotions and develop a positive attitude and vision for myself in life. In order to achieve success, you need to learn to be your own best motivator and believe in yourself.

Develop a set of personal rules. I decided to add a section to the back of my trading plan called 'Personal rules'. This is a list of bullet-point affirmations, quotes from successful traders and reminders to myself of my visions and goals in trading and in life. I cover this section of the trading plan in chapter 23.

Surround yourself with positive people who believe in you. It goes without saying that we are who we attract. In order to remain motivated and positive, we need to be with these kinds of people.

Be passionate about what it is you are doing and why you are doing it. You must have clear goals and understand your reasons for trading. Not only are persistence and determination keys to success, but you must be passionate about what you are doing. When you love doing something, you will persist with it.

Undertake regular exercise. There is a lot of truth in the saying that a 'healthy body keeps a healthy mind'.

3. Regularly evaluate yourself

Measure your performance in the markets. Trading is a probabilities game and you need to ensure the odds are in your favour. I regularly study and evaluate my performance—I examine my trading returns, reliability, average win size to average loss size, average hold time and equity curve (all of which are covered in chapter 21). It was the results of these measurements that made me realise I was sabotaging myself in the market with my options trading. I decided to change my trading style from short-term trading and focus instead on medium-term trading.

Understand what is working and stick with it. By measuring my performance in the markets I realised that I had been trading shares successfully, but I had given back these profits (plus extra) in trading options. I knew that I needed to take action and change my trading strategy. My goal was to get back on track with my trading and turn my equity curve around to a rising one with small drawdowns. So I spent time reworking my trading plan and developed a system that mostly involved trading shares and CFDs.

4. Manage your risk

Management of your trades is key. With every trade you undertake in the stock market, you are opening yourself up to risk. You are the only person who can control this. I never had a problem exiting my trades and was always disciplined at acting on my stop losses. However, sometimes I exited pre-emptively in expectation of my stop being hit, which prevented me from letting my profits run. In spite of this weakness, I know that money management has been my key to survival in the markets. Even though I overtraded and had a lot of open risk, it was the fact that I still limited my losses by acting on my initial stop loss that allowed me to survive the markets in my first year of full-time trading.

The key to controlling risk in the market is to use some simple money management techniques, which are covered in chapter 14.

Consistency is important. Once you have found a trading technique that works for you, stick to it and become consistent in the way you trade. For me, trading is a routine activity. I love the markets and love watching patterns unfold, but overall it is just a set of rules that I follow. I use MetaStock charting software to undertake searches for entry triggers and eyeball the charts looking for a desirable set-up (based on my set of rules). Then, if it all lines up, I enter the trade. After that, it is a matter of monitoring the market and managing my positions through my money management rules. To become successful and take the emotions out of trading, you must make your trading systematic.

5. Continue to educate yourself

Never stop learning. I view every trade I undertake in the markets as a new learning experience and I will never stop learning. In my early days of trading I made it a habit to regularly study myself and my trading systems. My aim was to continually build my instinctive mindset and gain confidence in my trading systems. As part of my trading routine each quarter, I would spend time studying the top winning and losing trades that my system generated, even those that I had not entered. I liked to study how the patterns in the charts unfolded and work out how I would have managed the trades if I had entered them. I also made it a rule to read one book about trading or personal development every month.

Consider finding a mentor. During the period in which I was self-sabotaging in the markets, I was highly influenced by other people and seminars that boasted that they could help me make large amounts of money per week or month trading. I realised that these seminars were not helping me and that they lacked a lot of quality and key information, especially those that promoted options trading.

I spent time seeking mentors who were honest in their approach and had trading styles that appealed to me. I discovered some mentors through reading their books, while others offered coaching and courses. My goal was to learn as much as I could from them in order to improve my trading skills, develop a mechanical trading system and improve my trading results.

Be disciplined and consistent

Trading is a psychological endeavour and it is what goes on inside your head that drives your market actions. Your goal is to take the emotion and guesswork out of your trading and aim to trade the market in a disciplined and consistent way.

The reality of trading

The reality of trading is nothing like you expect it to be and how a lot of seminars make it out to be. It is not until you invest your own money into the market that you become emotionally involved and you will be surprised by how this affects and clouds your vision—if you have not already experienced it.

Not every trade you undertake in the market will be profitable. There is no system that will produce 100 per cent winners and there is no Holy Grail or magical indicator. Most professional traders only win on 50 per cent of their trades. However, they know that the secret of success is about keeping the size of their winning trades much larger than their losing trades.

In order to build a profitable portfolio of shares, you need to be able to take losses. Unfortunately, you don't know which trades will be winners and you may have to enter a total of 10 trades just to create five winning trades. Your goal is to ensure your profits far outweigh your losses. This means you need to keep your losses low by exiting the trades that don't progress and holding on to the profitable trades.

What usually happens with beginner traders is they get frustrated with this process and become disheartened. They think their strategy isn't working and sell out of their five profitable trades to make up for the losses that they've taken. This makes them feel better and maybe they break even on all the trades. However, what they don't realise is that if they had let those five profitable trades run, they might have been surprised by the results. Because not every trade will be a winner and in order to build a profitable portfolio, you may need to take a series of losses first. Your losing trades should have a much shorter hold time than your winning trades—stick with the trades that are performing and get rid of the ones that are not.

Be aware that this is the reality of trading and this is how it all begins—don't get disheartened when you take your first loss. Just realise that the market is giving you your money back so that you can take on a better opportunity and get closer to that next big winning trade.

Trading is psychological

Trading the stock market is a great experience for personal growth. You will confront your own demons and you will hear that little voice inside your head that will put you down. It will tell you that you are not worthy, that you can't trade the markets, that you don't have what it takes and other silly thoughts. When you can overcome these hurdles in your mind and trade the stock market in a disciplined way by following a sound trading plan, you will grow tremendously.

> ### ✔ Smart action step
>
> Start a trading diary and record the thoughts and emotions that you experience each day. At the end of each week, review what you have written and determine if there are any patterns or bad habits that are limiting your trading potential and look at ways of overcoming these. Consider seeking help from a mentor or source books that will assist you to become a better trader—see the resources section in appendix B for recommendations.

3

Technical analysis overview

Technical analysis has become more popular than ever with the availability of computers, highly sophisticated charting software and the internet.

I am a technical trader and a big fan of charting. I make all my trading decisions using charts and I want to provide you with an overview as to what technical analysis is all about and why I love it so much.

First of all, let's review the two types of analysis that you can use to select shares. Then we will look at some basic charting analysis techniques that technical traders use to assist them with their trading decisions.

Fundamental versus technical analysis

There are two types of analysis that can be used for share trading: fundamental and technical analysis.

Fundamental analysis

This type of analysis is based on the use of economic data and company statistics to forecast prices. It involves reviewing company balance sheets, profit and loss statements and really studying the company, its management and its competitors to determine the actual value of the share. If you enjoy reviewing figures and interpreting data, then this type of analysis may suit you.

Technical analysis

Technical analysis involves reviewing actual price and volume activity of a share using charts, which helps to determine the best time to buy and sell a share. Markets move in trends and by understanding how shares trend you can determine the overall health and possible future price direction of a share by viewing its chart. A technical analyst studies the way the buyers and sellers are reacting to a share through its price movements, rather than studying the company itself.

Technical analysis can be used alone or in conjunction with fundamental analysis.

Which method of analysis is best?

Neither, because it comes down to personal preference.

Personally, I found fundamental analysis to be too time-consuming—I don't have the time to get to know such a large number of stocks. There are about 2000 stocks in the Australian market and even if you decided to just focus on the top 200 or 300 stocks, it would still be very time-consuming. I really like the idea of technical trading, where you determine the health of a share through its chart. The idea is to stay with a share while it is healthy and sell it when you see signs of the share becoming unhealthy. I believe charting is an extremely valuable tool—if you know how to use it.

Below is some information that will give you a basic understanding of technical analysis and reading charts. If you like the idea of technical analysis and want to learn more, visit <www.smarttrading.com.au> for more information—I would recommend the Smart Technical Analysis Home Study Course.

Charts

Technical analysis involves viewing charts of shares to make all your trading decisions. A share's chart is based on the price activity of that share. This activity includes the date, the opening price, closing price, highest price and lowest price of the share for that trade day and the volume traded.

You will need a computer and access to the internet to view charts. You can view them through many websites or through the use of specialised charting analysis software. This software is outlined in chapter 6.

Time periods

Charts can be viewed in a variety of different time periods, such as daily, weekly, monthly or quarterly. The daily chart shows each plot based on one day's price activity — its opening price, closing price, high and low price for the day and number of shares traded. A weekly chart compresses the daily price data into one week. The open price on a weekly chart will be the open price at the start of the trading week and the closing price will be the last traded price for the share on the last trade day of the week. The 'high' price is the highest price the share traded for during the week and the 'low' is the lowest price the share traded for during the week.

The charting period you select depends on the type of trader you are. For example, short-term traders usually focus their attention on daily charts, medium-term traders look at daily and weekly charts and long-term traders tend to focus more on weekly and monthly charts.

Types of charts

Charts can be displayed in many different ways. The three most common types are line charts, bar charts and candlestick charts. I personally prefer and use candlestick charts — all the charts that are displayed in this book will be in a candlestick format.

Line charts

Line charts, as shown in figure 3.1 (overleaf), are the simplest form of charting and often appear in the media when a chart of a share or index (for example, All Ordinaries or Dow Jones) is displayed. They show a single line that is plotted and joined based on the closing price of the share or index.

The disadvantage of these charts is that they only display the activity of one part of the market action, the closing price. Line charts do not take into account the opening price or the high and low price of the share.

Figure 3.1: example of a line chart

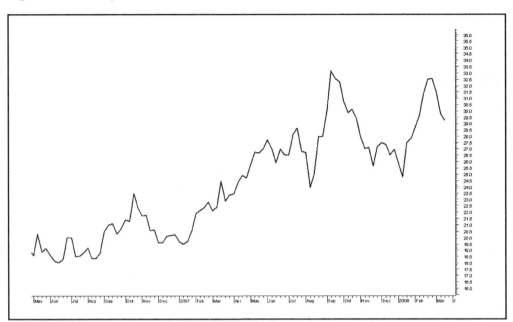

Bar charts

Bar charts, as shown in figure 3.2, are the charts most commonly used by technical traders. The chart is made up of a series of price bars that show all the price activity for the share. Each bar displays more than just the closing price — it also shows the highest price for the period, the lowest price and the opening price.

The only problem with viewing bar charts is that it's not easy to tell at a glance if the share increased in price for the day. If you use a charting software program you can set the bars to different colours — you can set all 'up' days to green and all 'down' days to red. Alternatively, you can use candlestick charts, which are my preferred chart type.

Figure 3.2: example of a bar chart

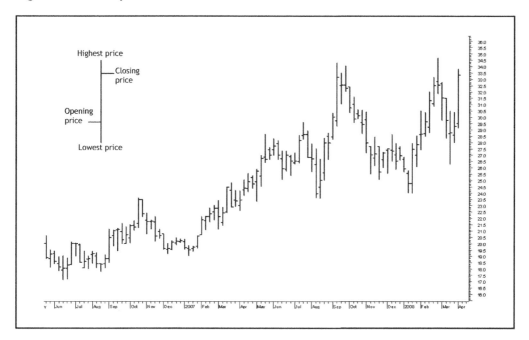

Candlestick charts

Candlestick charts, as shown in figure 3.3 (overleaf), were developed by the Japanese in the 17th century to analyse the price of rice. They display the same information as a bar chart, but in a more visual way. The difference is that the open and the close are connected with a white or black rectangle (candle body), and the highest and lowest price for the share appear as wicks protruding from the body of the candle.

The candle body between the open and closing price is coloured depending on how the share closed for the day. If the share rises, closing higher in price than it opened, it will be displayed as a white candle. If the share falls, closing lower in price than it opened, it will be displayed as a black candle.

Figure 3.3: example of a candlestick chart

If you turn back now and have a look at the previous two example charts in the line style and bar style, you will see that they all look very different. If you choose to use technical analysis, you will need to decide what type of chart you would prefer to use.

How to use technical analysis

Technical analysis is used to identify a range of factors to assist you with your decision making. They include:

- identifying significant reference points such as support and resistance areas
- identifying trends and determining if a share is in an uptrend, downtrend or sideways trend.

Significant reference points

Significant reference points are the support and resistance lines (or zones) that can be identified on charts. The reason they are significant is that they are trigger points that people remember, as they are the points where they started making or losing money.

Support lines

A support line is a significant price point that the share price consistently falls to before bouncing off and moving higher. It has the following characteristics:

- The share price can keep falling back to this point time and time again before it eventually takes off. It is like a floor in the chart, where there is buying support (possibly only temporarily). There are enough buyers at this price to stop prices falling further.

- Support lines are drawn on charts by connecting two or more 'price lows' with a horizontal line, as shown in figure 3.4. Connecting the price lows is just like joining the dots.

- The more often a share falls and bounces away from a support line, the more important that level of support becomes in the mind of the market.

If the share breaks through a significant support line, this is a negative sign for the price of the share, as it has now broken through its floor and could continue to fall. Figure 3.4 shows this occurring. The share breaks through its support line in mid December and falls significantly.

Figure 3.4: example of a support line

Resistance lines

A resistance line is a significant reference point that the price consistently rises to and then falls away from. It has the following characteristics:

- It is a level where there are sufficient sellers to stop the price rising any further. It is called a resistance level because the line acts as a barrier (or roof) to price advances.

- The level of selling taking place at this price level means that every time the share price approaches this particular line it is overwhelmed by sellers, temporarily halting the price advance.

- Resistance lines are drawn on charts by connecting two or more 'price highs' with a horizontal line, as shown in figure 3.5.

If the share breaks above a significant resistance line, it is a very positive sign for the price of the share because it could continue to rise.

Figure 3.5: example of a resistance line

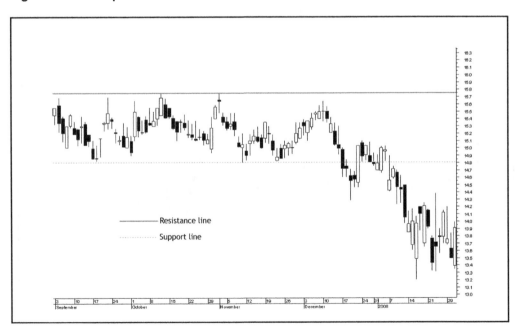

Change of polarity

Support and resistance levels can change roles. Resistance levels often become new support levels once the share price breaks above this level, as shown in figure 3.6. Likewise, support levels can often become new resistance levels, once the share price breaks through the support line.

For example, a share may try several times to move past a resistance level, but sellers come in and cause it to fall away from this price time and time again. Eventually, the share will gain enough momentum and break through the resistance level and surge to a new high. When this occurs, the line of resistance has been broken. Prices may fall back to this level and bounce, changing the resistance level to a support level.

Figure 3.6: example of a change of polarity

Once the share passes a significant support or resistance level, it often continues in the new direction until it reaches another line of support or resistance. If the share moves to new all-time highs (or virgin territory), then there is no resistance level preventing it from rising higher. It is in fresh territory until profit taking occurs in the market and it creates a new resistance level.

Trend identification

A common and wise proverb is 'The trend is your friend—never trade against the trend'. If you follow the trend of a share, and trade in that direction, you have a greater chance of success than if you trade against it.

A trend can be an uptrend, a downtrend or a sideways trend. As with support and resistance levels, trends are significant reference points that are drawn from either the price highs or lows on a chart. The only difference is they are drawn diagonally, showing where the price received support in an uptrend and where it found resistance in a downtrend.

A trend can be short or long in duration, lasting from only a few days to a number of years. The longer the timeframe of the trend, the more significant it is for the share price.

Uptrends

Uptrends can be identified by the following characteristics:

- Prices are continually rising, creating a series of higher highs and higher lows (as per figure 3.7).

- The buyers are evidently in control. Uptrends exist when the buyers outweigh the sellers, pushing the share price to higher and higher prices. They will continue to exist while buyers are plentiful and new buyers continually enter the market, purchasing the share and driving prices higher.

- There are usually a lot more white candles (rising candles) present in the chart during uptrends.

- Uptrends are drawn on the chart by joining the price lows with an upward-sloping diagonal line—connecting the lows from left to right, as shown in figure 3.7.

Uptrends can also be referred to as bullish trends, or bull markets. You may also hear traders talk about 'trading long'. This means they are buying the share or trading an instrument that will allow them to profit in a rising market.

Figure 3.7: example of an uptrend line

Uptrend line drawn diagonally
from the price lows

Downtrends

Downtrends can be identified by the following characteristics:

- Prices are continually moving downwards, creating a series of lower highs and lower lows.

- The sellers are evidently in control. Downtrends exist when the sellers outweigh the buyers, pushing the share price to increasingly lower levels.

- There are usually a lot more black candles (falling candles) present in the chart during downtrends.

- Downtrends are drawn on the chart by joining the price highs with a downward-sloping diagonal line—connecting the highs from left to right, as shown in figure 3.8 (overleaf).

Downtrends can also be referred to as bearish trends or bear markets. You may also hear traders talk about 'trading short'; this means they are short selling the share or trading an instrument that will allow them to profit in a falling market.

Figure 3.8: Downtrend line drawn diagonally from the price highs

Sideways trends

Sideways trends can be identified by the following points:

- They occur when the share is consolidating and is not reaching higher highs or lower lows. It trends between a strong support level and a strong resistance level for some time.

- This situation exists when the buyers and sellers are in equilibrium and neither group is dominant. Every time the share price rises to a certain level, sellers take profits, causing it to fall back again to around the same level. Buyers then re-enter the market and buy more shares (because this is where they made money last time they bought), and then sell when the price nears the same level again.

- These trends are hard to trade and there are not usually any clear trading signals given. It is best to wait until a breakout occurs and prices rise above the resistance level before taking any action.

- A sideways trend is like a pressure cooker waiting for something to happen. Either the buyers or the sellers will eventually become dominant and push prices in a new direction by breaking either the support or resistance level.

Figures 3.5 and 3.6 (on pages 20 and 21) contain good examples of sideways trends, where the share trended between support and resistance lines before eventually breaking through and starting either an uptrend or downtrend.

Why technical analysis?

I am a technical trader and I make all my trading decisions from charts. I am not concerned with the financial position of the company or other economic issues and I don't read the finance news or consider the company fundamentals. I use charts to show me the health of a share through identifying its trend. Just like a doctor can determine your health through blood test results, I use charts to do the same for a share. They tell me when it is the right time to buy and when it is time to sell.

In summary, the reasons why I prefer technical analysis are:

- The chart tells me the overall health of the share by how it is trending. I don't worry about news, fundamentals and announcements because financial markets have already responded to this information well before you read about it in the press. The market moves based on the future (rather than on current) earnings of a company.

- The data used in fundamental analysis can be six months out of date. Charts show the change in the trend of a share, well before any relevant fundamental information is available to the public.

- Shares such as One.Tel and HIH Insurance were being recommended by fundamentalists and brokers for a long time before they disappeared off the stock market. They were thought to be cheap and undervalued, yet these shares continued to fall and were eventually removed from the stock market as they became insolvent. For technical traders, the signs were clear in the charts that these shares were unhealthy and a clear exit signal was given a year or more before they became insolvent. Figures 3.9 and 3.10 (overleaf) show the charts of these shares—as you can see, they were clearly in long-term downtrends for more than a year before they were delisted from the stock market.

- Fundamental analysis does not take into account the underlying psychology of the market—it is people who make and move markets. The chart gives you an insight into how traders are thinking—whether they are excited or nervous and most of all if they are committed to the trend of the share. You can use these insights to make your own trading more profitable.

- I believe technical analysis gives me an edge in the market—it not only provides me with signals of the best time to buy, but most importantly it identifies the right time to exit, which is one of the most important and difficult parts of trading.

People tend to overcomplicate trading. In essence, it is simply about trading in the direction of the trend.

Figure 3.9: weekly chart of One.Tel

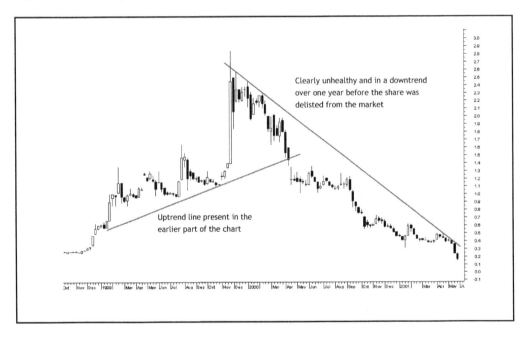

Clearly unhealthy and in a downtrend over one year before the share was delisted from the market

Uptrend line present in the earlier part of the chart

Figure 3.10: weekly chart of HIH Insurance

Support line evident. Share breaks
below this, which is a negative sign

Uptrend line present in earlier
part of the chart

Clearly unhealthy and in a downtrend
for three years before the share was
delisted from the market

✔ *Smart action step*

Understanding the basics of technical analysis can greatly assist you in your
share trading. You will discover how to read the health of the markets through
charts and know when it is the right time to buy and sell, plus much more.
You can learn more about technical analysis by visiting the resources section
in appendix B. Additionally, visit <www.smarttrading.com.au> for further
information about technical analysis.

Part II

Trading plan: the foundations

4

Goals and objectives

The first section of your trading plan is the fun part. This is where you can really get excited about why you are trading and give your trading purpose and a clear focus.

If you are not the type of person who sets goals for yourself, you may be inclined to skip this section of your trading plan and move on. I encourage you not to do so, because this is a very important part in your trading plan — it sets the scene for your trading and gives it direction. As a trader you are responsible for all your decisions and actions in the market. Successful traders have sound business plans with clear goals and objectives, setting out why they want to be a trader and what they are trying to achieve.

Remember the oft-quoted statistic that 80 per cent of traders fail to make money in the markets. If you want to be in the small percentage that is successful, then you need to be determined and passionate about achieving this. Now is your opportunity to really think about why you want to be a trader and what you want to achieve. Most people only have a vague and misty concept about the things they want and the clearer your vision, the more power you give to your desires and motivation to achieve them.

I always found that when things were not going well with trading, I could simply open up my trading plan and read this section. It would bring back all those feelings of why I want to trade and revitalise my focus to continue and learn from my current experience.

In this first section of your plan, you need to consider why you want to be a trader, set some clear goals as to what you want to achieve, understand what your trading 'edge' is and consider what your desired trading returns and objectives are.

Why am I trading?

So why do you want to be a trader? Having a plan is all about creating a vision statement as to why you want to trade the markets. A cornerstone of all successful businesses is a vision statement. It provides the business and its employees with an overall direction and focus. Now is your opportunity to create your own personal vision statement.

The statement will be individual and should be a source of motivation both now and in the future. Remember, trading is a serious business and the excitement will wear off when you hit that first cluster of losses. It is this section of your trading plan that will refocus you and remind you why you are trading. I recommend reading this section of your plan often, or even printing it out and keeping it by your computer. When you experience those days, weeks or months in which you think the entire market is against you, reread your vision statement and remember why you are doing this and decide if this is still what you want to do.

Christopher Tate, an Australian author and private trader, formulated the following questions in his book *The Art of Trading* (2nd edition). They will assist you in putting together your vision statement.

- *'Why do you want to be a trader?'* Yes, we are all trading for wealth creation, but there is usually some other underlying motives as well that motivate you to trade and be in control of your investments. Maybe it's the challenge of learning a new skill, a change in lifestyle or because you want to have control and make your own trading decisions in the market.

  I was determined to learn to trade and had a driving passion to become a trader. I wanted to create a lifestyle for myself where I could stay at home with my kids and bring in an income. I wanted to be able to watch them grow up and not have to put them in day care five days a week while I worked full-time.

- *'What do you think being a trader will bring you?'* It may bring you an income, it may not—it all depends on how disciplined you are and the risks you take. Maybe you are doing it so that you can work from home. Maybe you think trading will bring you freedom, but then again, maybe it will not. Trading can be a lonely endeavor.

The fast-paced world of day trading with a mob of traders yelling in one room is gone. Everything these days is computerised and you can trade from the comfort of your own home. Most of the time it is just you and the computer, which can be very lonely. The reality of trading is hard to imagine until you actually try it for yourself.

There is no doubt that trading is tough. It takes courage and discipline to stick with it during the hard times and ensure you don't overtrade and undertake large risks that will jeopardise your business of trading.

- *'What are you willing to risk to achieve your goal?'* Trading is hard work and takes time to learn. If you are not willing to put in the time and develop a well-defined trading plan, you won't succeed. The fact that you are reading this book suggests you must be ready to go that extra step and treat it like a business. Successful traders put the time in to get their trading businesses off the ground.

Figure 4.1 shows a sample vision statement from a trading plan. These samples are a guide only and have been included to assist you in completing each section of your trading plan.

Figure 4.1: sample vision statement from a trading plan

Why am I trading?

I am trading as a means to increase my net worth. It puts me in control of my wealth creation and offers me the opportunity to live a comfortable lifestyle. It is something that I am passionate about and I am prepared to put in as much time and dedication as is required to succeed.

Goals

Now that you have put your vision into words and written down why you want to be a trader, you need to be more specific and consider what your goals are as a trader. Goals are important because they give you direction and set guidelines around what you are trying to achieve and how you plan to do it.

Ask yourself what you plan to do to ensure you achieve your goal of wanting to be a successful trader. Think about the following questions:

- *What skills will you need to acquire to win the trading game?* You need to have a set of rules that set out how you are going to play the game. Just like in a game, sometimes you will win and sometimes you will lose. The goal is to win by a much greater amount than you lose. That's what's going to make you a successful trader.

- *What type of market analysis will you use to make your trading decisions?* Do you plan to use fundamental analysis, technical analysis, or a combination of both? An overview of the difference between these two types of trading methods can be found in chapter 3.

- *Do you plan to manage your ongoing risk in the market?* In order to be a successful trader you have to manage your risk. I cover strategies on how to do this in chapter 14. You don't want to be taking risks that will put your trading business in jeopardy.

- *Do you want to be consistently profitable?* Of course you do—what a silly question. But the reality is that you are going to take trading losses, because they are an inevitable part of trading. In order to survive and profit in the market, the goal is simply to keep your profits much larger than your losses.

Figure 4.2 shows a sample set of goals from a trading plan. Goals are individual and will vary widely between traders. It is important that you set goals that are achievable rather than impossible.

Figure 4.2: sample goals from a trading plan

Goals

My goals as a trader are to:

- become the best trader I can possibly be

- push myself forward and acquire the essential skills and psychological stability to conquer the trading game; this will involve taking occasional losses and having to confront my fears

- use technical analysis to assist me in my trading decisions and develop a long-term trend-following trading system

- manage my risk and protect my capital with the long-term goal of being consistently profitable

- give back and support the community; as my trading profits increase, I plan to donate a percentage of my profits to a chosen charity each year.

Trading edge

'If 80 per cent of people fail as traders, what makes you smarter, sharper, more intuitive or more disciplined than those who fail?' This is the question Christopher Tate poses in his book *The Art of Trading* (2nd edition), and it is the answer to this question that will determine your trading edge.

Trading is a serious business and all successful traders understand what their edge is in the market. Your emotional state is vital to your success as a trader. It is important that you understand what your psychological strengths and weaknesses are in relation to trading. The goal is to really get to know yourself and work on improving your performance in the market—just like a top athlete continues to train and focus on becoming a peak performer in his or her field.

You may not be aware of your strengths and weaknesses until you start trading and you may need to take steps to become aware of them as they occur. Your trading experience will be your best source of education in learning about yourself, because your emotions will become involved once you have your money in the market. You may have already felt these emotions and know that they can make you do things you shouldn't.

In chapter 2, I shared my trading journey with you and described the steps I undertook to get back on track and become the successful trader that I am today. These steps assisted me in getting to know myself and my weaknesses and allowed me to build strengths and create an edge in the market.

If you haven't read this chapter I suggest you go back and read it now and put a strategy in place to assist you in creating the winning mindset you need to be successful in the markets. Make it a goal to start a trading diary, source books on self -development, regularly evaluate your trading performance, manage your risk in the market and focus on improving your trading skills with education and practice.

Figure 4.3 provides a sample trading edge statement to guide you in documenting your trading edge in your plan.

Figure 4.3: a sample trading plan entry outlining an investor's trading edge

Trading edge

I believe my edge in the market is my trading strategy and personality. My trading strategy focuses on long-term trends and using money management strategies to protect my capital and let my profits run. It will be my determination, focus, motivation and organisation that will ensure I stay focused on my goals and aim for success in the markets.

Trading returns and objectives

Setting clear trading returns and objectives is a key element of any trading plan. They provide a benchmark against which you can measure your performance and your business. You may aim to achieve a set percentage or to outperform a specific market benchmark.

The big question is: what return is realistically possible with trading? There is no definitive answer to this, because everyone's trading methods are different. It is best to base your benchmark return on the current market environment, because market conditions will vary from year to year.

Your first goal as a beginner trader should be to survive. You want to protect your capital so that you can play the trading game long enough to learn the ropes and become consistently profitable. In order to do this, it is important to put strict money and risk management strategies in place. I cover these strategies in chapter 14.

Once you have proven that you can preserve your capital, aim for a more reasonable rate of return. To make trading worthwhile, you need to achieve at least a higher rate of return than a term-deposit account. There is no point in risking your money in the market if you can't exceed this benchmark. A term-deposit rate is a risk-free rate of return, guaranteed for a fixed term and requiring no effort on your part. The rate will vary from bank to bank based on capital and the fixed term, but it's a good benchmark against which to measure your performance.

Having goals to survive and then to outperform the term-deposit rate are achievable and valid objectives. Then, as you gain confidence (and develop a clear system that you adhere to), benchmark against the market you are trading. For example, if you are predominantly trading the Australian sharemarket, you can use the All Ordinaries index as a benchmark and make it your goal to outperform this index each year.

Table 4.1 shows changes in the All Ordinaries index over the past five financial years. As you can see, it has performed strongly for the past four years and provided returns near and over 20 per cent per annum. It also shows that every trading year is different—there can be years when the market provides a negative return. Over the long term, however, it was positive—the average return for these five years was 15.34 per cent per annum.

Table 4.1: percentage change in All Ordinaries index

Financial year	Growth in All Ords
2006–2007	25.35%
2005–2006	19.04%
2004–2005	19.80%
2003–2004	17.75%
2002–2003	−5.22%

To assist you in completing this section of your trading plan, ask yourself the following questions:

• *What percentage return are you expecting to make per annum?* Is there a specific and achievable return that you wish to net each year? You may decide instead to aim to outperform a set benchmark index, as already discussed.

• *Are you being realistic about the percentage return, or are you expecting to trade like the best trader in the world?* If you are expecting to make 50 per cent return on your capital, you are probably being unrealistic and putting undue pressure on yourself. The more pressure you put on yourself, the more emotional you become, the more mistakes you are likely to make and the harder the trading returns are to achieve.

- *Do you need to live off the money that you are using to trade?* If so, how much do you need to make on that money each year? In your first few years as a trader, it may be preferable if you have another source of income.

Personally, I don't set an exact percentage return that I want to make each year, because every trading year is going to be different. My personal goal is to outperform the All Ordinaries every year. If the All Ordinaries rises by 20 per cent, I want to do better than that. So whatever the change in the All Ordinaries, whether it be positive or negative, I want to outperform this benchmark in positive returns each year.

Figure 4.4 shows some sample objectives that beginner traders may include in this part of their trading plan. Depending on your experience, how much capital you have and your acceptable level of risk, this could vary greatly.

Figure 4.4: sample trading returns from a trading plan

Trading returns and objectives

I will trade the Australian stock market through shares and aim to achieve the following:

Year	Goal
One	To survive
Two	To generate a higher rate of return than a term deposit
Three and beyond	To outperform the All Ordinaries each and every year

✔ Smart action steps

- Now is the time to think about your goals for your trading business and create a vision statement.

- Think about both your personal and financial objectives and start documenting them. Open your *Smart Trading Plan Template* and go to the first section, called Goals & Objectives. Type in your thoughts and answers to each of the questions.

- I suggest you come back to this section in a few weeks and review what you have put together and change it if necessary. Print out this page and put it next to your computer to remind you about why you are trading. It will help you to refocus when times get tough in the market.

5

Trading structure

Now we are getting down to the serious side of trading. One of the first major business decisions you will need to make is deciding on the most appropriate structure for your trading operations. It's important to choose the business structure that best suits your needs and personal circumstances.

Business structures

The five most common business structures in Australia that can be used for trading and investing are:

- sole trader

- partnership

- company

- trust

- self managed superannuation fund (SMSF).

The main reasons for choosing a particular structure would be for tax purposes and possibly asset protection. The costs of setting up and maintaining the structure will also affect your decision. Here are some factors that will require your consideration:

- the establishment costs to set up the business

- the ongoing costs for maintaining the business—annual fees, administration fees and accounting costs to maintain the appropriate records

- the allocation of funds to operate the business

- the method by which the business pays you an income

- the tax requirements and benefits for the business

- the GST requirements for the business

- the method by which the business will protect your assets

- the accounting and record-keeping requirements of the business

- the responsibilities in operating the business

- the legal liabilities of the business

- the method by which the business is wound up.

Seeking professional advice

Deciding on the best structure can be a difficult decision and it is important that you seek professional advice from an accountant.

Your personal circumstances

To advise you on the best structure for your business, your accountant will need to understand your personal situation. The sort of information the accountant will require to assist you in making this decision will be:

- your personal tax situation—how you pay tax and your tax bracket

- the amount of capital you will be trading

- your trading objectives

- the expected income from your trading

- your family situation and the income levels of family members

- your age

- the risks of the trading business

- your financial situation

- your goals in protecting your assets.

Finding a good accountant

It is very difficult to find a good accountant and it is wise to choose carefully and ensure you find someone you can trust. As you can see from the list above, you will be providing your accountant with private records and personal information that you wouldn't necessarily want anyone else to see or know about.

If you don't have or know of a good accountant the best place to start is to ask around. Ask your friends who they use and if they recommend them. If you have a trading mentor or have met a group of traders or investors through your trading journey, ask them who they use. Reputation is a good indicator of ability.

If no-one is able to confidently recommend an accountant, then call a number of local accountants in your area and interview them over the phone. Ask them a range of questions, including relevant personal questions. You want to use an accountant who practices what he or she preaches. It is always great to find one who is also an investor. Here is a list of questions you might like to ask:

- What qualifications do you have?

- Are you a member of any professional accounting bodies?

- Do you specialise in a particular area of tax?

- Do you set up a lot of business structures?

- Do you personally invest in the stock market?

- What business structures have you set up for your personal investments?

- Do you think asset protection is important and should be considered when deciding on the best structure?

- What accounting software do you use and support?

- How do you charge for your services?

- Can you tell me why I should use you as an accountant?

Ensure they answer your questions clearly and don't beat around the bush. You want to ensure the accountant appreciates your circumstances and communicates well. There is nothing worse than accountants who use a lot of jargon and talk themselves up. Personally, I like to get to know my accountant and feel comfortable talking about my personal circumstances. I always make sure I understand what he or she is telling me.

When you select an accountant, don't automatically choose the one with the cheapest fees. You want the accountant who offers the best service that meets your needs and understands what you are looking for. It can be very expensive to change your set-up, so it is better to get it right from the very start rather than hire the cheapest accountant and act on bad advice.

Overview of the different structures

You must thoroughly understand the structure you choose and ensure it is cost effective, meets your goals and objectives and, most importantly, is flexible enough to suit your personal circumstances—allowing you to make changes based on your circumstances if need be.

It is always good to do some background research on the different structures available before you raise the topic with your accountant. Below is an overview of the different structures and a brief list of some of their advantages and disadvantages. You will need to discuss your personal circumstances with your accountant, because he or she will make a recommendation based on your individual situation.

Sole trader

Sole traders are individuals who operate businesses for themselves, either in their own names or in registered business names. The businesses have no separate legal entity and the income and expenses are taken into account in the owner's personal tax. It is a simple business structure that provides owners with the flexibility of all the decision making and financial management.

Table 5.1 outlines the advantages and disadvantages of working as a sole trader.

Table 5.1: sole trader

Advantages	Disadvantages	Other information
It is the simplest and most inexpensive structure to set up and maintain	The business has no separate legal entity from the owner	It uses an individual tax file number
All profits and capital belong to the sole trader	There is no asset protection; the sole trader has unlimited liability. This means that he or she is personally responsible and liable for all debts. Personal assets can be used to pay for the business debts	Sole traders need to register for an Australian Business Number (ABN) from the tax office
Business losses can be offset against any other income earned	Capital is limited by the sole trader's personal assets	Sole traders must register for GST if the business's annual turnover is over a certain amount each year
The sole trader has full control over the management and direction of the business	The business is reliant on one person and is affected by absences such as illness or holidays	Sole traders may need to operate within the Pay As You Go (PAYG) instalments and/or PAYG withholding systems. This means the trader will be required to pay PAYG instalments through the year towards his or her expected income tax liability
The sole trader owns all the assets of the business (which may be a disadvantage if he or she wants to protect those assets)	There are no tax-minimisation strategies. The sole trader must pay tax on the whole taxable income of the business and it is added to his or her personal tax return—it cannot be split with a spouse or family members	—

Table 5.1 *(cont'd): sole trader*

Advantages	Disadvantages	Other information
It is easy to wind up and change the structure at any time	The business terminates on the death of the sole trader	—
There is little paperwork and fewer government regulations concerning business operation than with other structures	—	—

Partnership

A partnership can be formed when two or more people (up to 20) go into business together, in either their own names or in a registered business name, with the view of making a profit. It is important that all partners know their rights and responsibilities and they are all willing to work towards the same goal.

Partnerships are regulated by the Partnership Act and an agreement is made between the interested parties. This agreement can be verbal or in writing, but it is best if a written partnership is put in place with the assistance of a solicitor.

Table 5.2 outlines the advantages and disadvantages of working in a partnership.

Table 5.2: partnership

Advantages	Disadvantages	Other information
Easy and inexpensive structure to set up and maintain	No separate legal entity from the partners	Partners need to apply for a tax file number
Tax advantages—income is split between partners (based on each partner's percentage share set out in the partnership agreement)	No asset protection: each partner has unlimited liability for all financial obligations and debts of the business—personal assets are at risk	If using a registered business name, partners need to register for an ABN from the tax office

Advantages	Disadvantages	Other information
Shared responsibility and risk in operating the business reduces individual burdens, making it easier to take time off	Personality clashes and problems can arise if the relationship between partners is unsuitable and this can affect the decision making and management of the business	Partners must register for GST if the annual turnover is over a certain amount each year
Access to a range of knowledge, experience, skills and possibly additional capital from all partners	No tax-minimisation strategies — each partner pays tax on his or her share as an individual and is taxed at personal tax rates	Partners must lodge an annual partnership income tax return to show all income and expenses incurred in carrying on the partnership business
Fewer government regulations in operating the business than some other structures	Partnerships terminate on the death or resignation of a partner	—
Easy to wind up and change the structure at any time	—	—

Company

A company is a complex business structure that is formed by one or more people who want to have a business that is a separate legal entity to themselves. It has different profit distribution, taxation and legal responsibilities than a sole trader or partnership.

It is set up with a minimum of one shareholder who owns the company and one director who manages the company. The director can also be a shareholder in the company. Companies are registered under Corporations Law and regulated by the Australian Securities & Investment Commission (ASIC). The set up and administrative costs are usually higher than those of other business structures.

Table 5.3 (overleaf) lists the advantages and disadvantages of a company structure.

Table 5.3: company

Advantages	Disadvantages	Other information
Separate legal entity in its own right—business name is registered nationally and has a legal status across Australia	Companies are complex business structures that are costly to set up and maintain. It has ongoing ASIC administrative costs and extra accounting costs	Companies are given an Australian Company Number (ACN) when they are set-up and this must be shown on all documents
Shareholders have limited liability based on the amount they paid for their shares	Directors have substantial obligations, responsibilities and record-keeping requirements under Corporations Law and ASIC. Fines and penalties are payable if obligations are not met	Owners must apply for a tax file number
Offers a greater level of asset protection as personal assets are separate from the business and may be protected from business risk, unless they have been personally used to guarantee debt	Termination of business can be costly and complex	Owners must register for an ABN from the Tax Office
Shares are transferable and it is easier to bring in new shareholders and attract capital for the business	Income earned by the business belongs to the company. It can only be paid to shareholders, directors and employees in the form of PAYG income or dividends	Owners must register for GST if the company's annual turnover is over a certain amount each year

Advantages	Disadvantages	Other information
Possible tax advantages — company tax rates apply, which is a flat rate (30 per cent at the time of printing this book) that is less than the highest individual tax bracket. Profits are not required to be distributed and can remain in the company	—	Owners must lodge an annual tax return to show all income and expenses incurred in carrying on the business and the company's income tax
Shareholders can also be employees of the company and gain the benefits that come with employment	—	Owners need to open a separate bank account and keep all the company's assets separate from personal assets when managing income and expenses
Business is not terminated by the death or bankruptcy of a shareholder	—	Companies usually operate within the PAYG instalments and/ or PAYG withholding systems. This means the PAYG instalments are paid throughout the year and credited against the annual income tax liability of the company

Trust

A trust is a business structure that is administered by a trustee (a person or a company) who holds the property of the trust and earns and distributes its income on behalf of the beneficiaries. Instead of shareholders, a trust has beneficiaries who are entitled to distributions of income. These distributions are controlled by the trustee and form part of the beneficiary's personal income. They are subject to personal income tax.

This type of business structure is formed by a 'settlor', who makes a gift or settlement (in the form of money) to the trustee on behalf of the trust. A solicitor then issues a trust deed that sets out the trust's powers and formalises its administration. One of the most common types of trusts is a discretionary (or family) trust.

Table 5.4 outlines the advantages and disadvantages of operating as a trust.

Table 5.4: trust

Advantages	Disadvantages	Other information
Greater flexibility in the distribution of income and capital	It is a complex business structure that is costly to set up and maintain	It is best to establish a trust deed with the help of a solicitor
Tax-minimisation advantages—income can be distributed to spouse and family members in such a way as to minimise tax	Difficult to close down or dismantle	Trustees must apply for a tax file number
A trustee can be a company, providing limited liability and asset protection to the trust's property	A trust deed has a limited life	Trustees must apply for an ABN from the Tax Office
Beneficiaries' assets are protected from business risk	The trust must be run according to the rules of the trust deed and changes may be required to the deed before certain activities can occur	Trustees must register for GST if the trust's annual turnover is over a certain amount each year
The structure can be used as an estate-planning tool	Losses remain in the trust and are offset against future income—they cannot be distributed	Trustees must open a separate bank account and keep all the trust's assets separate from personal assets when managing income and expenses

Advantages	Disadvantages	Other information
Trusts are not terminated on the death of a beneficiary	All profits must be distributed to beneficiaries. Otherwise, they are taxed at the highest marginal rate	Trustees can register for PAYG if applicable
—	—	Trustees must lodge an annual tax return to show all income and expenses incurred in carrying on the business and the amount of income distributed to each beneficiary

Self managed superannuation fund

More and more Australians are now choosing to manage their superannuation funds. This means that you set up your super fund as a self managed superannuation fund (SMSF). An SMSF is a small superannuation trust (made up of fewer than five members) with the sole purpose of providing retirement benefits to its members, who act as trustees to the SMSF. Managing your own fund gives the owner greater control and flexibility over its investments and discretion, but it is costly to set up, with annual fees and strict responsibilities.

Table 5.5 outlines the advantages and disadvantages of operating as a self managed superannuation fund.

Table 5.5: self managed superannuation fund

Advantages	Disadvantages	Other information
Lower tax rate on income and contributions and opportunity to manage the tax of the fund effectively	Money and assets in the super fund are locked in and cannot be distributed to the trustees until they are over the retirement age set out by SMSF	A trust deed must be established, requiring review and updating every few years

Table 5.5 (cont'd): self managed superannuation fund

Advantages	Disadvantages	Other information
Assets are protected in the super fund	Strict responsibilities and rigorous record-keeping involved. Approved auditors and tax agents audit the fund annually and prepare the annual tax return requirements	The SMSF must be registered with the Australian Tax Office and trustees must apply for a tax file number and ABN
Trustees have complete control over the fund and its investments and can pick and choose their own strategy and investments (within the legislative framework)	Trustees are fully responsible for all the decisions and obligations of the fund and must ensure compliance with the superannuation laws. Trustees may be penalised for breaches of the law	The SMSF must be registered for GST if its annual turnover is over a certain amount each year
SMSFs can provide a range of options in terms of benefit payments and estate planning	Trustees should have adequate financial knowledge or use a financial adviser to assist in running the SMSF, because government legislation on SMSFs changes regularly	Trustees must open a separate bank account and keep all the SMSF's assets separate from personal assets when managing contributions, investments, earnings and expenses
No management fees	Establishment and ongoing costs are high and may not be cost-effective if the total fund assets are under $100 000. Additional ongoing costs include auditing, tax return admin and annual levies	Trustees are required to prepare and implement an investment strategy for the fund that controls the way contributions are invested. They must take into account a range of factors such as risk, return, diversification, liquidity, cash flow and asset allocation

Advantages	Disadvantages	Other information
—	Money cannot be borrowed on behalf of the SMSF	An accountant is required to prepare the fund's annual report, financial statements, members' statements and tax return. The SMSF must be audited by an approved auditor
—	There are restrictions on the types of investments an SMSF can hold	—

Summary

There are quite a few structures to choose from and they all have their advantages and disadvantages. The structure you choose will depend on your own personal circumstances, your trading capital and the type of trader you want to be.

A trader just starting out with a small account may initially choose to trade in his or her personal name. A long-term investor who is nearing retirement may be interested in taking control of his or her superannuation fund. A trader with a large trading account in a high personal tax bracket may decide to set up a company or trust structure to trade under.

Seek the advice of an accountant before setting up a specific business structure. When you do select a structure, don't just accept what the accountant recommends. Ensure you are clear on why they are recommending that structure and it meets all your needs. If it is not clear, ask for more information. You want to know everything about that structure, how it will operate and what your responsibilities are in operating it.

Once you have decided on your structure, document this in your trading plan. Figure 5.1 (overleaf) shows an example of how you would do so.

Figure 5.1: example statement from a trading plan

> ## Trading structure
>
> At first, I will trade in my individual name. Once my account size and profits increase, I will seek the advice of an accountant to set up an alternative structure that suits my new requirements.

✔ Smart action step

Decide on a trading structure that best suits your requirements and (if need be) seek the advice of an accountant to discuss your options and assist in setting up the appropriate structure.

6

Trading tools

In order to trade the markets and manage your business of trading, you will require a range of equipment and resources. Every trader needs access to share prices and an account with a broker. If you are a long-term investor, this may be all you require, but if you are an active trader like myself, you will need much more.

Basically, trading tools are anything that you use as part of your business of trading—websites, newspapers, books, computers, software, data services, brokers and so on. It's a good idea to list all these tools in your trading plan.

Let's take a look at the different tools and equipment that you may require as part of managing your business of trading.

Computers

These days it is necessary to have a computer. If you are serious about your trading business then it is vital that you have one.

All my trading decisions are based on technical analysis, so my computer is used to view charts, run market scans and manage my business of trading. Most computers these days come with Microsoft programs and I use these to track and manage my trading. I use a specialised Excel spreadsheet to track and keep records of all my trading positions and I use Word to keep my trading plan up to date. If you have downloaded the *Smart Trading Plan Template*, it is set up in a Word format ready for your input.

When purchasing a computer, be sure to select one that is capable of running the software that you require for your trading business. Computers become out of date very quickly so it is always best to purchase the latest computer with the fastest RAM and largest memory capability to ensure that it will run the most up-to-date software.

Software

There are numerous charting packages available and you may have already heard of MetaStock, Incredible Charts, EzyCharts, Bourse, Bull Charts and Amibroker, to name just a few. As I have mentioned earlier, I use MetaStock—all the charts displayed in this book have been produced using MetaStock software.

Many websites offer the facility to view charts of shares, but they are often limited in functionality. Most online brokers allow you to view charts of shares on their websites. You can also use the free service websites that are available such as Yahoo Finance <www.yahoo.com.au/finance> and Trading Room <www.tradingroom. com.au>.

If you are interested in charting and want to trial a program before spending money on software, there is a free program available called Incredible Charts. You can download it from <www.incrediblecharts.com>. It performs most of the functions you will require and is a good start for beginner traders. If you are a long-term trader, it might be all that you ever need to use. If you decide you want to trade more regularly (and more actively) and you want to develop your own market scans and indicators, then you will require a program such as MetaStock. MetaStock is one of the more powerful charting programs on the market, but there are many others to choose from.

Charting packages fall into one of three categories—they are tool boxes, grey boxes or black boxes. This is determined by their functionality.

MetaStock is a tool box. Tool boxes come with a range of pre-coded indicators and scans, but their main advantage is that they give you the freedom to code them as you desire and create your own personal stock market scans and indicators— without limitation.

Incredible Charts, on the other hand, is a grey box. Grey boxes also come with a range of pre-coded indicators and scans, but there are limitations as to how far you can go with this software. For example, you cannot create your own indicators and the stock scans are limited to a set of tick boxes—you can't code beyond these parameters.

Then there are black boxes. There are a lot of black boxes on the market and they are usually sold for large amounts of money—anywhere from $5000 to $10000. They come with an entire education package and are pre-coded with a set system that provides buy and sell signals. You are not able to create your own systems and cannot do any more with them. Black boxes often fail to deliver because people don't have confidence in them and don't fully understand how they operate. This is because they didn't develop the systems themselves.

I wanted the freedom to be able to create my own trading systems and customise the software to suit, so I chose to purchase a tool box. After that, it was a matter of researching the different programs, exploring their capabilities and finding out what my mentors used to help me with my software selection.

Data providers

If you do purchase a charting program, you will also require a data supplier to provide you with the price and volume figures for all shares on the ASX each day. Your charting program will then add this data to its ongoing history and convert it into charts for you to view.

Data is the key component and the most important part of charting. There are a lot of data providers available, but not all of these are good quality. To be able to make accurate trading decisions in the market, you must ensure that you have a quality data supplier. If your data includes gaps, incorrect prices and does not adjust share prices when shares split in price, then you have bad data. Find a supplier that will guarantee clean and accurate data on a daily basis.

Make sure your data provider has a good history of error-free data and also provides custom folders. Custom folders are very important and not all data providers offer them. The benefit of having custom folders is that you can actually run a scan on a set selection of stocks (such as the S&P/ASX 200 or 300), or a selected market sector, and so on.

Be aware that your data provider will most likely offer you a range of data packages. You will be asked which stock exchange you want to receive data for and how often you want to receive that data—intraday, end of day or next day.

Having intraday data usually means that you can download the data hourly. End-of-day data is delivered at the end of each trading day and next-day data arrives the following day. Obviously, next-day data is much cheaper than intraday data, but your choice will depend on what style of trader you are. I use intraday data because I make all my trading decisions at 3.30 pm, half an hour before the market closes. If you work full-time and only get a chance to check the market in the evening, then end-of-day data may suffice. If you are a long-term investor and are only interested in checking the charts every few days, then next-day data would be suitable.

I personally use DataHQ (available from <www.smarttradingdata.com.au>) because the supplier has a good reputation for accurate data and it offers custom folders. Also, DataHQ is the only data supplier I am aware of that offers monthly subscriptions and you can upgrade and downgrade your subscription as required. Most suppliers offer annual packages.

Mobile phones and pocket watches

Nowadays you can have stock market data instantly available no matter where you are. Portable devices such as pocket watches and mobile phones enable you to check stock market prices, receive alerts and even place trades in the market. Trading can be as active and portable as you want it to be.

I use my mobile phone as a trading tool when I go on holidays. Before I leave, I arrange to have my portfolio sent to my phone as an SMS message at the end of each trading day. I can also log onto the internet on my mobile to check my portfolio or a particular share and also arrange for a text alert message if a share I own hits my stop level. I can then ring my broker or set automatic stop losses in the market. Stop losses are covered in chapter 15.

If you do want to be able to access stock market information on your mobile or another type of portable device, ensure you purchase a brand and model that enables you to do so. Do your research, decide what functions you want and seek out a product that has the right capabilities. Obviously there will be costs involved in using these services and you will need to decide if these ongoing costs are worthwhile.

Sources of information

As a minimum, you must have access to daily share price information. Some traders prefer more detailed information on the day's market action, latest news and other events related to the stock market or particular shares. This information can be obtained through many sources, such as:

- newsletters from brokers or other financial services

- share or financial magazines

- newspapers and television

- websites.

Obviously, some of the data sources will be more up to date than others. Depending on what type of trader you are, you may or may not require access to the very latest information.

Newsletters

There is so much data available on the stock market that it is very easy to get bogged down with too much information and subscribe to too many newsletters. Newsletters are usually in electronic format and are either free or subscription based. I can't vouch for any newsletter services, as I don't personally use them. I use charts to make all my trading decisions and source further information from my broker's website.

Magazines

There are some great share magazines that you can subscribe to, such as *Your Trading Edge*, *Personal Investor*, *Shares* and *BRW*—just to name a few. They all provide excellent information, education and share analysis. My personal favourite is *Your Trading Edge* <www.yte.com.au>—it's a strategy-based magazine that specialises in trader education.

Newspapers and television

Most daily newspapers have a financial section with a summary of share prices and business news. The evening news on television also reports on the financial markets, although the information is always after the event and is usually 'old news' by the time the program goes to air.

Websites

The internet is the most popular source these days for stock market news, but be aware of where the data comes from. When you use Google to search for information on a company it will bring up a number of sites, ranging from the company's own website to news reports and chat room blogs. There are a lot of trading chat rooms around, but don't waste time on them—there is no way of knowing the credibility of the person you are chatting with. Chat rooms are also a big time-waster—time that could instead be used in developing your own personal trading system and writing your trading plan.

The information I source from my broker's website includes upcoming dividend information, indices and the industry sector the share belongs to, current market depth and volume for the trade day. There is also a range of fundamental information available and regular announcements and news updates. If your broker does not offer this information then you may consider sourcing it from other websites. I have used the two websites below for many years and they are definitely worth checking out. I have listed other relevant websites in figure 6.1 on page 62.

- <www.tradingroom.com.au>—this is the Fairfax Digital trading information website. It provides 20 minutes delayed data, but you can simply register for free to receive access to the live data and other share information. It includes a wealth of information on shares and financial markets and is a good place to start if you don't have a trading account and you are keen to source daily share price and market information.

- <www.asx.com.au>—this is the Australian Securities Exchange website. It also contains a wealth of information on the Australian stock market, ranging from share price and news information to education and even trading games. A few times each year the ASX runs sharemarket games that provide a great way to build your confidence in the market and to practise your trading skills. All you need to do is to register before the next game is scheduled to run and you will be given a hypothetical bank account to trade over a few months. These games give you a good feel for what real trading is all about.

Brokers

In order to be able to trade the stock market you must have an account with a broker. This can be a discount broker such as Commsec or E-trade, that usually offer online trading and voice broker services. If you like the idea of having your own dedicated broker to look after you personally, you may prefer to set yourself up with a full-service broker (although their services will cost more). Keep in mind that there are no guarantees on a broker's advice. You need to determine what sort of service you are looking for and seek a brokerage firm that offers this.

Just like seeking an accountant, it can be difficult to find a suitable full-service broker. Ask around for a recommendation and interview a number of brokers before setting up an account. Ensure you understand the brokerage fees, the bank account you are required to have in order to trade, the services they offer, how they source their fundamental information, facilities available on their websites and how your account will be handled when your dedicated broker is ill or away on holidays. Most importantly, ensure your orders are executed efficiently and that you receive instant confirmation of your trades.

As I make all my own trading decisions in the market, I prefer to trade using an online discount broker. I have an account with a broker for trading shares and one for trading CFDs (contracts for difference), which are covered in chapter 8.

Trading library and education

There is a wealth of information on trading and thousands of books and courses available on the topic—too many in actual fact—and not all are worthwhile. Every book store has a financial section with shelves dedicated to the stock market and that is probably how you purchased this particular book. It's easy to get bogged down with too much information, making it hard to know where to start.

Decide on the trading method you want to use, such as technical analysis or fundamental analysis, then focus on books on these topics. Once you find a book you like, check the references at the end, as they usually include the author's favourite books—just as I have included my favourite books in the resources section at the back of this book. Over time, you will build up your own personal library and have a selection of favourites that you can refer to from time to time.

Some of the books I have included in appendix B may be hard to source. The website that I have found to be the best supplier of trading books is called Moneybags <www.smarttrading.com.au/books>. It specialises in trading and investment books and you can order online and have your books delivered directly to your door.

Your goal is to continually improve your trading performance in the market and continue to develop your trading skills. Make education part of your trading routine. This could involve reading a book on the markets or personal development once a month or undertaking a new course each year. Visit <www.smarttrading.com.au> for more information on the courses I offer.

Figure 6.1 is a sample list of trading tools from a technical trader's plan. Study this list and then compose your own.

Figure 6.1: sample list of trading tools from a trading plan for a technical trader

Trading tools

- I will use MetaStock software to view charts and scan the market for trading opportunities. The stock market data will be provided by DataHQ <www.smarttradingdata.com.au>.

- Microsoft software, such as Excel and Word, will be used for gathering trading notes. I will use the *Smart Trader Spreadsheet* <www.smarttrading. com.au> for tracking and managing my trades.

- A range of websites will be used to view share price and market action:

  » My broker's website will be used to view market depth, trade shares and review upcoming dividends.

  » The Trading Room website <www.tradingroom.com.au> will be used as a backup to view share price information and market news.

  » The ASX website <www.asx.com.au> will be a source of information on the Australian stock market.

  » The *Australian Financial Review* <www.afr.com.au> will be a source of market news and financial information.

  » Yahoo finance <www.yahoo.com.au/finance> will be another source for market news and financial information.

- Other websites of interest:

  » Nasdaq <www.nasdaq.com> will be used to view the US stock market performance.

> » Stock Charts <www.stockcharts.com> will enable me to view technical charts of US stocks and indices.

> » Kitco <www.kitco.com> will be a source of information and charts of gold and other precious metals.

- I have selected _____ as my broker for trading shares.

- I will use a mobile phone to manage my portfolio through SMS and wireless internet, especially when I am travelling.

- I will build up a library of educational books on trading that are recommended by authors and other traders I know. I will regularly attend courses to educate myself on the business of trading.

✔ Smart action step

If you have not done so already, write out a list of all the trading tools you will need in order to start your trading business. Ensure you check out the resources section at the back of this book for more recommendations.

Part III

Trading plan: methodology

7

Trading style

Determining which trading style to adopt is an essential decision when preparing a trading plan. You need to consider what timeframe you want to trade, because being a day trader is very different to being a long-term investor. It is all about how frequently you want to trade and how long you would like to hold trades open for. There is no right or wrong—the style you select must be one that you are comfortable with and that suits your personality and lifestyle.

I have tried all styles of trading and experimented with a range of different instruments such as CFDs, options and warrants (I cover these instruments in detail in chapter 8). It was part of my trading journey and I needed to try them out to discover which style suited me.

Firstly, let's take a look at the different trading styles and then explore how to determine which style suits you.

Different trading styles

Trading falls into three categories: short term, medium term and long term. To better understand which style you would select, let's take a look at the advantages and disadvantages of each one.

Short-term trading

Short-term trading is when you hold a trade anywhere from a few minutes to a few days. Day traders also fall into this category. A day trader only keeps trades open during the trading day and has no trades open overnight. A short-term trader, on the other hand, would hold positions overnight and may continue to hold them for a few days. Short-term trading requires the ability to monitor the market for most of the day and is more suited to people who trade the markets full-time or work part-time outside market hours.

If you plan to trade short-term, select a trading instrument that is highly liquid and has good volatility. This may be a share or a derivative instrument such as options or CFDs. 'Highly liquid' means the instrument must have a high turnover during the day. There are a lot of buyers and sellers available and the buying and selling prices are close together. This makes it easier for short-term traders to enter and exit very quickly.

Volatility refers to price movement. Short-term traders are interested in instruments that have a high volatility, meaning they have good price movement between their high and low price during the day, making it possible to make money in a short space of time. The best way to understand a share's volatility is to look at its average true range. This is a technical indicator that can be used to measure the average daily movement of a share. I cover this indicator in detail in chapter 12.

To determine whether you are suited to short-term trading, consider the following advantages and disadvantages:

Advantages:

- Because they do not hold positions overnight, day traders are not exposed to movement in overseas markets. They are not affected by how the market opens the next day. The Australian market is affected by the performance of overseas markets. For example, if the Dow Jones fell by 2 per cent overnight, the Australian market will most likely fall when it opens, with shares opening much lower than the previous trading day. The opposite would apply if the Dow Jones rose 2 per cent overnight.

- Less equity can be used because short-term traders do not usually hold many positions open at once.

Disadvantages:

- Short-term trading requires close monitoring of the market. It is critically important to be able to monitor the market for most of the trading day with few interruptions.

- This style of trading is stressful because a lot can happen in a short space of time. You need to have the psychological makeup to cope with it (trading psychology is covered in chapter 2).

- There are additional costs for live data and for some news information. To be an effective short-term trader, you need the most recent data and thus require a trading platform that provides this. Another option is to have a pocket watch or mobile phone that is capable of providing live data when you are out and about (I discussed these portable devices in chapter 6).

- The brokerage costs are higher. While it is easier to negotiate cheaper brokerage costs when you are an active short-term trader, brokerage costs are higher due to the frequency of trades each day and these do add up over time.

- Closer stop-loss techniques need to be used and this means it is easier to be knocked out of trades prematurely. It does not take much for share prices to move to a stop point and be taken out of a trade. It can be frustrating to watch the share hit your stop and recover quickly. In these situations, you need to act fast to re-enter the trade.

- Large moves in a share price take time to develop and short-term traders can miss out on big profits due to the short hold time of their positions.

- Short-term traders take losses a lot quicker than others and can hit a cluster of losses in a row more frequently. You must be able to withstand taking losses and know when to quit if things are not going well during that particular trading day. It can be very easy to sabotage yourself with short-term trading. You really need to know yourself and know when it is time to stop trading for the day and start fresh tomorrow.

Medium-term trading

Medium-term trading involves holding a trade anywhere from a few weeks to a few months. This style of trading is often referred to as 'swing trading', because it involves taking a swing move within an overall trending share. For example, if a share is in an uptrend, medium-term traders will buy the share when it bounces off its trendline and ride the upward movement, exiting the trade when the share shows signs of falling back towards its trendline again.

Medium-term traders do not need to monitor the market as actively as short-term traders; they only need to check it in the evenings or a few times throughout the day. This method of trading suits people who don't have much time during the trading day to focus on the markets.

Advantages:

- This style is less stressful and time-consuming than short-term trading. It may take time to learn and develop your trading style, but once you have a routine in place it is less time-consuming, because you do not need to watch the market all day long.

- Medium-term traders use wider stop-loss techniques than short-term traders. They give the share more room to move, which provides the opportunity for a larger profit on a single trade.

- Business costs are lower because you will not require live market data and information.

Disadvantages:

- Medium-term traders often have a lot of positions open at one time. This means higher brokerage costs and a larger equity base.

- You can still miss out on the very large moves. Shares can rise in price for long periods of time and medium-term traders may not hold trades long enough to make the large profit returns on a single trade that long-term investors can achieve.

- Medium-term traders may get knocked out of trades prematurely when they fall back in price and then rebound and continue higher. Because the stop losses employed are usually not wide enough to hold you in the long-term trend of the share, this can be frustrating at times. You need to be more active and re-enter trades when you receive another signal.

- Medium-term traders hit a cluster of losses a lot quicker than long-term traders. They need to be able to handle this and know when it is time to take a break.

- Medium-term trading is difficult during sideways trends or directionless markets that continue for long periods of time and can be very frustrating.

Long-term trading

Long-term trading is also referred to as 'buy and hold' and suits investors who want to retain a share for a long period of time with the goal of receiving an income from dividends and enjoying the benefit of large capital gains. It is the least stressful and time-consuming style of trading and is often referred to as investing.

Investors usually use either technical or fundamental indicators to determine when to exit. Investors who use technical analysis aim to buy stocks that show signs of being in an uptrend and remain in that trend until they get a signal of a trendline break. This could take anywhere from a few months to years.

Advantages:

- This style of trading is much less stressful and less time-consuming than other styles. You only need to track the markets once a week and do not need to check the market during the trading day.

- It is very cost effective because no live market data and news services are required.

- Brokerage costs are low because you do not trade very often, so your turnover of trades is not as high.

- Wide stop-loss techniques are used to enable investors to hold a share for the long term. Some people use no stop losses at all and will hold shares no matter what happens. Personally, I would not hold a position without a stop loss, no matter what timeframe I was trading.

- Investors make large profits on single trades because they give trades a lot of room to move and hold trades for a longer period of time, making it possible to achieve 100 per cent returns (or higher) on a single trade.

- Investors can build on positions that are profitable by purchasing more shares as they continue higher in price.

- Long-term investors have the benefit of receiving regular dividend payments.

Disadvantages:

- It requires patience and discipline to stay with trades for the long term and not to react too quickly and take profits. You need to let the market unfold and use wide stop losses in order to hold trades for a long period.

- Long-term trading requires a larger capital base that can be left invested in the market for a longer period of time.

Determining your trading style

To help you decide on the best style to focus on, consider the following questions:

- *How much time during the day can you devote to trading while the market is open?* Do you have a full-time job and plan to only check the markets in the evenings? Or do you have a flexible job that allows you to review the market regularly during trading hours? Or can you devote yourself to full-time trading and watch the market all day?

  You really need to consider how much time you have available each day. If you want to be an intraday trader, you have to sit in front of a computer for most of the day and you don't want to be interrupted too often.

- *How many distractions do you face during the trading day?* If you plan to be a short-term day trader then you need to ensure that you do not have too many distractions. If you do, think about ways to overcome these distractions.

- *How long do you want to keep your trades active for?* You can keep trades open anywhere from just a few minutes to a few months or longer. You need to consider if you want to trade short term or use a buy and hold strategy and retain your trades for the long term.

- *What type of instrument do you want to trade?* Different instruments have different timeframes and some require closer monitoring than others. For example, options require close monitoring because they have expiry dates and are short term in nature, whereas shares can be held for as long as you like. These instruments are explored further in chapter 8.

Ask yourself how much time you have to devote to trading and consider the advantages and disadvantages of the different trading styles and instruments. This will help you determine what sort of trader you want to be.

So which style to choose?

You can make trading as active and demanding as you want it to be. Would you be happy to sit in front of a computer screen for most of the trading day, watching the market activity minute by minute and placing orders seconds after you get a signal and then exiting promptly when the trade becomes unfavourable? Or would you prefer to check the market once a day and place your trades the following day if you get a signal? Or maybe you would prefer to only trade once a week? This is something that you need to decide for yourself—it will come down to how much time you have to devote to trading and what your psyche can handle.

Remember, there is no right or wrong. Just because someone trades actively all day, undertaking 20 trades in a week, does not mean he or she will make more money than someone who trades once a month. People think that the more often you trade, the more money you will make. The reality is that there are many wealthy long-term traders out there. Short-term trading is not for everyone, but some people love it. Personally, I wouldn't want to be stuck in front of my computer watching the market all day. It just does not suit my lifestyle, especially now that I have two young children.

Sometimes the best way to learn is to slow down and build your confidence in the market first. It might be best to focus on a long-term system to start with. Your trading costs will be lower, you will spend less time on trading and you can focus on learning and developing your trading plan. Then, as your knowledge and confidence increases, you can incorporate a medium- to short-term system to complement your long-term trading.

Remember, there is no hurry. The market will be open five days per week for your entire life. People tend to forget this fact and start trading too early because they are scared of missing out—I know I did. When you have decided on a trading style that suits your psychology, the time you have available to trade and the instrument you will be trading, remember to document the style in your trading plan.

Figure 7.1 provides a sample statement from a trading plan to guide you in preparing your trading style statement.

Figure 7.1: sample statement from a trading plan for a long-term investor

> ## Trading style
>
> I will focus on long-term investing in the Australian stock market. I am a trend follower and my plan is to seek out rising shares, build a profitable portfolio and gain additional income through dividends. I will use technical analysis and let the charts tell me when the trend is over and it is time to exit.

Once you have decided on a trading style, you can select an instrument that suits your trading timeframe, which is what the next chapter is all about.

✔ Smart action step

Decide on a trading style that best suits your personality and lifestyle. Consider the questions in this chapter when deciding which style to focus on.

8

Trading instruments

Selecting an instrument that suits your trading style is a critically important decision. A trading instrument is an asset or contract with monetary value that can be traded between two parties. They include anything from shares to CFDs (traded in a simulated market) to derivative instruments (such as options and warrants), available for trading in the Australian and international markets. It is important to note that different instruments have different timeframes and some require closer monitoring than others. Thus, your choice of instrument will link closely with the trading style you have chosen and the time you have available to trade.

I've traded many different instruments and timeframes over the years, from day trading to short-term trading with options, warrants and CFDs with varied results. I eventually settled on a medium-term and long-term trading style, predominantly trading shares and share CFDs with consistently profitable results and a much better lifestyle to boot.

Let's have a look at some of the different trading instruments available, what style of trading they are suited to and their advantages and disadvantages. You can find out more information on any of the instruments through the ASX website <www.asx. com.au>. Also refer to the resources section at the back of the book for recommended books and websites.

Shares

Shares are also referred to as stocks, securities and equities. A share is a small holding of a company that you can buy either privately or through a listed company on the stock market. For the purpose of this book I am referring to shares as those bought through the stock market.

To buy a share you need to have an account with a stock broker—this could be a discount broker that offers online trading and voice brokering services or it could be a full-service broker who you deal with personally and who provides advice if required.

Shares can be traded by any style of trader—short-, medium- or long-term traders.

Advantages

Trading shares has the following advantages:

- Shares are the most favourable instrument for tax advantages because there are tax credits on most dividends in the form of franking credits and a discounted capital gains tax rate.

- They provide excellent returns for long-term investing because they have no expiry dates and can be held for as long as the company is listed on the stock exchange, which could be for a lifetime.

- Shares are easy to buy and sell if you are dealing with liquid shares (meaning the shares have a good turnover each day and there are always plenty of buyers and sellers available—liquidity is covered in more detail in chapter 13).

- Share traders can easily diversify between a range of different sectors or industry types.

- Shares include voting rights and entitlements to shareholder discounts or incentive benefits if they are available.

Disadvantages

The disadvantages of trading shares include the following:

- Companies can go broke and enter into receivership, leaving shareholders with a worthless holding. That is why it is important to diversify and have an exit strategy when things are no longer favourable. Technical analysis will show signs of unhealthy shares well before they go into receivership and are delisted from the stock market (see charts of One.Tel and HIH Insurance in figures 3.9 and 3.10 in chapter 3).

- Share trading requires a large capital base in order to be able to diversify in the marketplace.

Contracts for difference (CFDs)

CFDs are becoming increasingly popular because they offer many benefits that the stock market does not. A CFD is a contract between you and the company that you are using to make the purchase. You trade the same shares as with the ASX, but in a simulated market environment. If you were to buy 1000 National Australia Bank CFDs, you would have a contract with the CFD provider for that trade. A shareholder, on the other hand, actually owns a stake in the company.

In short, a CFD offers the benefits of trading shares by mirroring the performance of the share or index, without the need to actually own them.

There are some specialist providers in Australia that only offer CFD trading, and more and more brokers now offer CFD trading along with share trading. Be aware that the brokers don't necessarily offer the same facilities as specialist CFD providers.

CFDs suit short-term and medium-term trading due to the interest component that is payable on trades that remain open overnight and for longer periods of time.

Advantages

CFD trading has the following advantages:

- With the power of leverage, you can trade CFDs with margins from as low as 3 per cent to as high as 50 per cent.

- Traders can earn interest through short selling. This is a strategy used to trade falling shares and it is covered in chapter 16.

- Traders can access a wide range of global markets with most major CFD providers.

- Traders can trade a range of instruments including share CFDs, foreign exchange, indices and commodities, all with one provider. This means it is easy to diversify between a range of different sectors or industry types, as well as different markets and instruments.

- CFD traders can set guaranteed stop loss orders (GSLOs). As per their name, these stops are guaranteed and you will be exited out of a trade at the exact price you set, no matter what the share price does. This is not possible in the real market. Stop losses are covered in chapter 15.

- Trading CFDs is similar to trading shares because they have no time component and are not as complicated as trading options.

- Dividends are paid on share CFDs (although no franking credits are included).

- Like shares, CFDs are easy to buy and sell if you are dealing with liquid CFDs.

Disadvantages

CFD trading has the following disadvantages:

- Traders are required to pay interest on a daily basis for all CFD positions held overnight.

- CFD traders have no voting rights or entitlements to shareholder discounts or incentive benefits.

- CFDs carry no franking credits on dividends.

- There is only a small range of share CFDs available for trading. Depending on the provider, you may have access to anything from 50 to 500 share CFDs.

- Leverage is also a disadvantage because it is very easy to trade well beyond your means and wipe out your trading capital in a short space of time if you are not careful. This can be overcome with the use of GSLOs.

Options

Options are derivative instruments that enable traders to buy or sell shares in the future, depending on whether the option is a call or a put. Call options enable traders to profit from share price rises by buying shares at a set price (known as the strike price) by a set future date (known as the expiry date). For example, if you were to buy a $30 call option on ANZ, you are buying the right, but not the obligation, to purchase ANZ shares at the price of $30 by the expiry date of the option. On the other hand, buying a put option enables you to profit from a share price fall by giving you the right (but not the obligation) to sell ANZ shares at $30 by the expiry date.

Options are most suited to short-term trading because they are highly leveraged instruments and have an expiry date. They therefore need to be monitored intraday. Options can be traded with full-service brokers and most discount brokers.

Advantages

Option trading has the following advantages:

- Options are highly leveraged instruments that provide exposure to shares at a fraction of the share price. For example, an option may cost $0.50 while the share itself may cost $30. They are usually traded in lots of 1000 units (which is one contract), so one options contract at $0.50 per option would cost $500 (1000 × $0.50) whereas buying 1000 shares at $30 would cost $30 000. Be aware that options have a limited life, because they have expiry dates. The closer to expiry the option is, the cheaper it is to purchase.

- There is limited risk involved. The total amount that you can lose is limited to the options price paid when the trade is opened.

- There are multiple ways to trade options. They can be traded as individual instruments, sold to create an income on your portfolio (known as options writing), used to purchase shares at a set price (call options), used to hedge shares that you own (put options), as well as other strategies, ranging from conservative to high risk.

- Options traders can ride volatility movements by buying when the volatility is low and selling when it rises.

Disadvantages

Options trading has the following disadvantages:

- Higher brokerage costs which can add up if you have a series of losing trades.

- Options have expiry dates and decay in value as they near these dates. Traders are therefore limited to short-term trades. Time stops are necessary to ensure the option doesn't expire worthless.

- Options are complicated instruments and you need to take into consideration volatility, strike prices, expiry dates and other components that make up their pricing before entering a trade. Make sure you understand how they work and put in extra time to work out which option to select.

- No dividends are paid on options.

- Option trading requires a great deal of monitoring.

- Options trading is not an orderly market like shares. You have to deal with the market makers and play the spread to place a trade. This can be frustrating and costly at times, because options tend to have wider spreads.

- There can be liquidity problems due to the larger range of different strike prices and expiry dates available, which can make trading options difficult.

- There is unlimited risk involved if you are an options writer and write uncovered options where you do not own the underlying share.

Warrants

Like options, warrants are derivative instruments. They are available in the form of calls and puts and will enable you to buy or sell shares at fixed strike prices by a set expiry date. The difference between options and warrants is that warrants are issued by financial institutions and are traded on the ASX, much like shares. Warrants are traded through either discount or full-service brokers with the same trading account that you would use to trade shares. With options, individuals can sell them and make a market (also known as options writing), but this is not possible with warrants.

There are three main types of warrants to choose from — trading warrants, instalment warrants and endowment warrants. They each have different conditions. Instalment and endowment warrants tend to be longer dated and are suitable for long-term investing, while trading warrants are relatively short dated and (like options) are more suitable for short-term trading.

Advantages

Trading warrants have the following advantages:

- Warrants have lower brokerage costs than options.

- Warrants have much tighter spreads and a more orderly market than options.

- A warrant is a highly leveraged instrument that provides exposure to shares at a fraction of the share price.

- There is limited risk. The total amount that you can lose is limited to the price of the warrant.

- Traders can hedge their portfolios through put warrants.

- Volatility is not an issue and does not need to be considered as it does with options. Warrants already have a high degree of volatility built into them, so you pay a higher price for that volatility.

Disadvantages

Trading warrants have the following disadvantages:

- Like options, warrants are restricted to an expiry date and can expire worthless if you take no action. This means you would lose the capital you invested, so a time stop is necessary.

- No dividends are paid on trading warrants.

- You cannot be a seller of warrants; only a buyer. It is a directional trading method only.

- Warrants traders cannot take as large a position as options trades because they are higher priced due to high volatility being factored into the price.

- Warrants don't offer as much choice as options with strike prices and expiry dates.

- Traders need to spend time educating themselves about the different types of warrants and understanding the components that make up the price of the instrument.

Which market?

Once you have selected an instrument, which market do you plan to trade? Do you want to trade the Australian market only, or overseas markets as well? Computerised trading has made it possible to trade any global market. For example, you could trade shares, CFDs or options in the US stock market, London, or Japan if you desire. Be aware that some overseas markets operate during our night time, so if you do decide to trade global markets you may need to be awake during their market hours, particularly if you are a short-term trader. This does not matter so much if you are a medium- to long-term trader.

Once you decide on your market, do you plan to limit yourself to a set area of the market? For example, you may prefer to trade only liquid shares and focus on the S&P/ASX 100 or 300 shares only. Or if you decide to trade short-term with options, you may decide to pick five blue chip shares that you will get to know really well and trade options over these shares only. There is no right or wrong.

Personally, I prefer to trade liquid markets that I know I can easily get in and out of. So I focus my share and CFD trading on the S&P/ASX 300 stocks of the market. I have always found plenty of opportunities in these stocks and I know it is very easy to exit a trade and get out at (or close to) my set stop loss.

Figure 8.1 is an example instrument statement from a trading plan for a long-term investor. Once you have determined the instrument or instruments that you will trade, document it in your trading plan. Remember to review your trading plan regularly because you may change instruments as your trading develops.

Figure 8.1: example statement from a trading plan for a long-term investor

Trading instruments

I have chosen to trade the Australian market only and focus on the S&P/ASX 300 shares to ensure sufficient liquidity and price discovery.

✔ *Smart action step*

Decide what markets and trading instruments you plan to trade to suit the trading style you have chosen. If need be, you can do more research into the trading instrument you have chosen by visiting the ASX website <www.asx. com.au>. You may need to seek out a company that offers this instrument. Ensure you understand all the conditions and features that the company you select offers for the instrument before opening an account.

Part IV ▲ Trading plan: indicators

9

Indicators

There is a large number of indicators for both fundamental and technical analysis. You need to decide which ones to use to assist you in making your trading decisions and narrow down your watch lists.

Technical indicators, such as moving average indicators, can be plotted on charts using software such as MetaStock. Figure 9.1 (overleaf) is an example of how a moving average indicator would appear when applied to the chart of a share using the MetaStock software. This indicator is discussed in more detail in chapter 10. Fundamental indicators are calculated using information from the company's profit and loss statements and the current share price information.

You may choose to use one type of indicator only, or you may choose to combine the fundamental indicators with a range of technical indicators to support your decision—there is no right or wrong. Once you have decided on your method of analysis, your trading style and the markets you are going to trade, ask yourself what indicators you will use to help with your stock selection process. These indicators will form part of your trading rules, covered in detail in chapter 18.

Figure 9.1: daily candlestick chart with 30-day moving average

Below is information on the range of indicators you can use, the most common indicators, and the indicators that I personally prefer.

Fundamental indicators

Fundamental analysis uses a range of key fundamental measurements along with other company information to assist in deciding which share is best to buy at the current time. The most common measurements are the price/earnings ratio and dividend yield. These measurements are most suited to long-term investors who are looking for value stocks with future capital growth and a good dividend yield. This information can be combined with technical analysis if desired.

Price/earnings ratio (P/E ratio)

A P/E ratio is calculated by taking the current share price and dividing this by its earnings per share (EPS) over the last 12 months. The EPS figure is provided by the company in its annual reporting and is generated by dividing the company's annual operating profit after tax by the number of its shares on issue. For example, if a share is trading at $30.00 and its EPS over the last 12 months was $1.50, the P/E ratio for the share would be 20 ($30.00 ÷ $1.50). This means that share owners are paying $20.00 for every dollar of earnings.

Companies that have negative earnings or no profit will have an undefined P/E ratio and will usually be shown as not applicable (or N/A). Such a company would not be an attractive investment.

The lower the P/E ratio in relation to the company's growth, the more attractive the company is to invest in because the chance of growth in the future is higher. If one share has a P/E ratio of 10 and the other (from the same industry sector) has a ratio of 40, then the share with the P/E ratio of 10 would be seen as more attractive. A technical trader would then check the chart to make sure the share is healthy by identifying if it's in an uptrend before buying in.

A low P/E ratio, however, does not automatically mean that a share is a good buy—it is not a ratio that should be used alone. It is a measurement that can be used in conjunction with others to assist in selecting between shares.

Dividend yield

The dividend yield of a company is calculated by dividing the total dividends of the past 12 months by its current share price. This is an important measure for long-term investors because it tells them the yield they will receive from their investments in the form of dividends. For example, if a share is trading at $20 and pays out dividends for the year at $1, then it has a yield of 5 per cent. This means investors will earn a total of 5 per cent on their investment in this company if they hold it over a period of a year. The higher the yield, the more attractive the share is.

Blue chip companies tend to have higher dividend yields because they are established companies. Most small companies will have no yield because they do not pay out a dividend. These companies like to keep their profits within the company to continue to fuel future growth and development and may pay out a regular dividend later down the track.

Investors who aim to build long-term portfolios with good dividend-paying stocks may have a rule that they will only purchase shares with a dividend yield above a set percentage. The dividend yield is not an indicator of future capital growth, but will indicate what shareholders will earn in income on their total investment. When deciding between two shares, if one has a dividend yield of 2 per cent and the other 5 per cent, an investor will most likely favour the share with the 5 per cent yield.

Technical indicators

Charting software comes with a large range of pre-packaged technical indicators to choose from and can be very overwhelming. There are also plenty of books about the different types of technical indicators and even an encyclopedia on the subject. You will come across many of these sources of information throughout your trading development.

Technical indicators used in charting are a mathematical calculation of the raw data; that is, the price and sometimes the volume. They are often referred to as price/volume indicators. Don't get too weighed down with indicators and use too many, because they will only confuse you. The best way to start is to consider what the indicators measure and to categorise them, then select one indicator from each category. Below is a list of the price/volume indicator categories and the indicators from each of these categories provided in MetaStock version 7.02. This shows you just how many indicators there are available in one charting package, although they will vary between different packages and software versions. I have put the indicators that I use from each category in bold, and discuss these indicators further in the following chapters.

Trend indicators

These indicators are used to identify the direction of a trend. Along with the use of trendlines and support and resistance lines (drawn on the chart to identify the trend of the share as discussed in chapter 3), there are indicators that you can apply to charts to assist you in confirming the trend. I use the moving average indicator to assist me in understanding the current trend of a share and this is covered further in chapter 10.

Aroon	Commodity Selection Index	DEMA	Directional Movement
Forecast Oscillator	Linear Regression Indicator	Linear Regression Slope	Linear Regression Trendline

MACD	**Moving Averages** (all methods)	Parabolic SAR	Performance
Polarized Fractal Efficiency	Price Oscillator	Qstick Indicator	r-squared
Raff Regression Channel	Standard Deviation Channel	Standard Error	Standard Error Bands
Standard Error Channel	TEMA	Time Series Forecast	Vertical Horizontal Filter
Zig Zag			

Momentum indicators

Momentum indicators measure the speed at which prices move over a set period of time. These indicators are popular and can be used for buy and sell signals as well as signals showing a weakening of the share's current movement. The momentum indicator I use is the MACD histogram, which I cover in chapter 11.

Accumulation Swing Index	Chande Momentum Oscillator	Commodity Channel Index	Dynamic Momentum Index
Intraday Momentum Index	Linear Regression Slope	**MACD**	Mass Index
Momentum Indicator	Price Oscillator	Price Rate-Of-Change	Random Walk Index
Range Indicator	Relative Momentum Index	Relative Strength Index	Stochastic Momentum Index

Stochastic Oscillator	Swing Index	Trix	Ultimate Oscillator
Williams' %R	Williams' Accumulation/ Distribution		

Volatility indicators

Volatility measures the fluctuations in prices (either up or down) over a set period of time. It helps you to understand the personality of the share, because some shares are obviously more volatile than others. It's important to understand the type of share you are dealing with. I have selected the average true range indicator from the list below as my chosen volatility indicator and this is covered in more detail in chapter 12.

Average True Range	Bollinger Bands	Commodity Selection Index	Moving Average (variable)
ODDS™ Probability Cones	Relative Volatility Index	Standard Deviation	Standard Error Bands
Volatility, Chaikin's	Volatility, Option		

Market strength indicators

Also called volume indicators, these indicators help to confirm the strength of the current trend of a share. All the indicators below incorporate either volume or open interest in their calculations, which are the key ingredients in measuring market strength.

The higher the volume or open interest for a share, the more participants there are behind the move and therefore the more strength. For market strength, I use the raw volume itself and I cover this in more detail in chapter 13.

Accumulation/ Distribution	Chaikin Money Flow	Chaikin Oscillator	Demand Index
Ease of Movement	Herrick Payoff Index	Klinger Oscillator	Money Flow Index
Moving Average (volume adjusted)	Negative Volume Index	On Balance Volume	Open Interest
Positive Volume Index	Price Volume Trend	Trade Volume Index	**Volume**
Volume Oscillator	Volume Rate-Of-Change		

Which indicator?

There are many indicators to choose from and you can use as many indicators as you like, although your choices may change over time as you learn more about technical trading.

Be aware that indicators are not 100 per cent accurate with their signals and they do fail from time to time. It's easy to get bogged down with learning about them all, making it hard to decide which ones to use in your trading. I know because I have experienced this myself.

This is because every book you read on technical analysis, including this one, will discuss the author's favourite indicators. Every author will prefer different indicators and discuss them in a way that will make you fall in love with them. I loved so many of them that I used to have a ten indicator entry checklist that I ticked off before I could open a trade. Only problem was that so many of the indicators conflicted with each other that I found it very hard to open trades that met all the indicator signals.

In the end, I went back to the basics and decided to take a simple approach and focus on the raw data with one indicator from each category.

Once you have decided on which indicators to use, document them in your trading plan. Figure 9.2 (overleaf) shows an example of how you may document these indicators in your trading plan.

Figure 9.2: example statement from a trading plan for a long-term technical investor

Indicators

To measure	Selected indicator
The trend	Trendlines, support/resistance lines, 30-week exponential moving average
Momentum	MACD histogram
Volatility	Average true range (ATR)
Market strength	Volume

✔ *Smart action step*

Review the list of indicators in this chapter and read the following chapters to help you decide which indicators to use to start with. Focus on selecting one indicator from each category.

10

Moving averages

A moving average (MA) is an indicator that can be applied to the prices of a chart to assist in confirming the trend of the share. It is basically a smoothed line that follows the share price.

It plots points on the chart to form a smoothed line by taking the sum of the closing prices and averaging them out. For example, a 30-day moving average takes the closing prices of the share for the last 30 days, divides this by 30 and plots it on the chart. Figure 9.1 on page 86 shows a sample candlestick chart with a 30-day moving average line plotted over the price of the share.

Types of moving averages

There are three types of MAs that can be used and each are calculated using different variations. They are called simple, exponential and weighted moving averages:

- *Simple moving average.* This is a simple calculation of the average price of the share. It is calculated by adding up the share's closing price for a selected period and then dividing this by the number of periods. This results in the average price of the share for the selected time period being plotted on the chart.

- *Exponential moving average (EMA).* This is calculated by applying a percentage of today's closing price to yesterday's MA value (based on the selected periods). This calculation method gives greater weight to the most recent data and less weight to earlier data and therefore reacts faster to changes in trend than a simple MA.

- *Weighted moving average.* The weighted MA is designed to give greater weight to recent data. It is calculated by multiplying each of the previous days' data by a weight and giving more weight to today's price and less to older prices. While it is similar to the EMA, it reacts much faster to changes in trend and can give false signals.

To better understand the differences between these three MAs, take a look at figure 10.1. This is a sample chart with the three MAs applied. When the share price is rising you can see the simple moving average is slower and sits further away from the share price. The EMA sits closer to the share price, reacting faster than the simple MA, while the weighted MA sits the closest because it reacts much faster again. However, it can also give false signals.

There is no right or wrong as to which moving average you select. I personally use the exponential moving average because most traders use this and it is a happy medium between the three different types.

Figure 10.1: weekly chart with the different MAs

Moving average timeframes

When you plot an MA on a chart, you need to select the timeframe (number of periods) you want to use. Different timeframes affect the appearance and signals generated by the MA.

The smaller the timeframe (meaning the lower the number MA) the faster the MA will move because it is closely linked to the price movements of the share. Fast MAs give a quick indication of a share price but are less accurate because they are too closely related to the share price.

The larger the timeframe (meaning the higher the number MA), the slower the MA. Slower MAs give a slower indication of price movements and tend to give a smoother line.

Figure 10.2 shows the variation between three different timeframe simple MAs. As you can see, the lower the number, the closer the MA sits to the share price activity. The five-day MA is much faster than a 30-day MA and this is faster than the 150-day MA, which sits the furthest away from the price activity.

Figure 10.2: daily chart with different period simple MAs

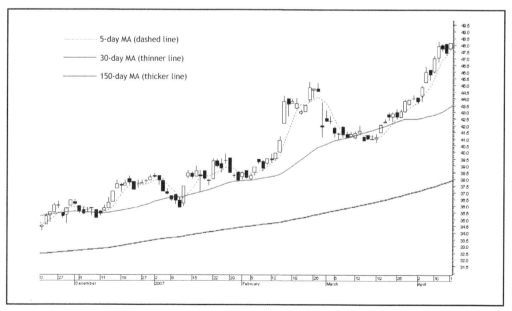

There is no ideal number MA and it is best to decide the MA timeframe based on the timeframe that you trade. You will probably need to experiment to find the best ratios that work for you. Use the following as a guide:

- If you are a short-term trader and trade shares or derivatives (options or warrants) from a few days to a week, it is best to apply a short-term MA of, say, five or 10 days (or both).

- If you are a medium-term trader and intend to hold shares for a few weeks to a few months, then a 30-day MA may suit.

- A longer term trader who intends to hold shares for a few months to possibly a year or more would use a long-term MA, such as 100 to 150 days.

These time periods relate to daily charts, but MAs can be applied to weekly and monthly charts too. A 150-day MA would be equivalent to using a 30-week MA on a weekly chart (based on five trading days per week).

How to use moving averages

MAs can be used in a number of ways, from singularly to in a combination. Used singularly, they act as support and resistance lines and determine the overall trend of the share. Combinations do the same, but they also provide buy and sell signals.

Single moving average

Long-term traders can use a single moving average to assist in confirming the trend of a share. One of the best methods is to apply a 30-week EMA to a weekly chart and use the direction that the EMA is moving to confirm the trend of the share. For example:

- A share is healthy and in an uptrend if its EMA line is rising and the share price is predominantly located above it.

- A share is unhealthy and in a downtrend when its EMA line is falling and the share price is predominantly located below it.

- A share is seen to be consolidating and trending sideways if the EMA line is flat and the share price is zigzagging above and below it.

Figure 10.3 shows a weekly chart with a 30-week EMA. The EMA is rising and the share price is predominantly above it, confirming that the share is in an uptrend.

Figure 10.3: weekly chart with a 30-week EMA

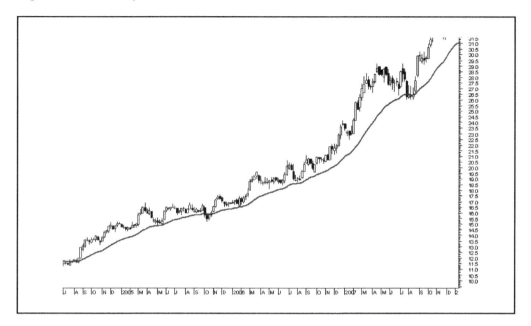

Combination of two moving averages

While a single MA provides you with a view of the overall trend of a share, some traders find that this is not enough and prefer to use a combination of two MAs or more. When using two moving averages in combination, you would use both a long-term and short-term MA. The long-term MA gives you a feel for the general trend of a share and generates trading signals when overlayed with a shorter term MA. These signals are summarised below.

- When the fast MA crosses *above* the slow MA, this signifies a change in trend and a possible start of an uptrend. Some traders use this as a buy signal to purchase the share.

- When the fast MA continues to stay *above* the slow MA, this confirms an uptrend.

- When the fast MA moves *below* the slow MA, this signifies a change in trend and the possible start of a downtrend. Some traders use this as an exit signal to sell the share.

- When the fast MA continues to stay *below* the slow MA, this confirms a downtrend.

These signals work well when the share is trending up or down. However, when a share trends sideways, the MA signals become unreliable because they crisscross frequently. During this time, it's better to use support and resistance lines (outlined in chapter 3) to define the trading range and wait for a break to occur above or below one of these lines.

Once again, the timeframe you trade will determine the combination of MAs you use:

- Short-term options traders would use two shorter MAs of, say, five and 10 days. Faster MAs are more responsive to short-term movements in the market.

- Medium-term share traders may use a combination of, say, 15 and 30 days, because they want a smooth, less responsive curve that will keep them in the trend for a longer period of time.

- A long-term trader would prefer a much longer term MA, or would use a weekly chart of two weekly MAs, such as a 15-week and 30-week MA.

Figure 10.4 shows how two MAs would appear on the chart of a share and the signals they generate.

Figure 10.4: daily chart with two MAs

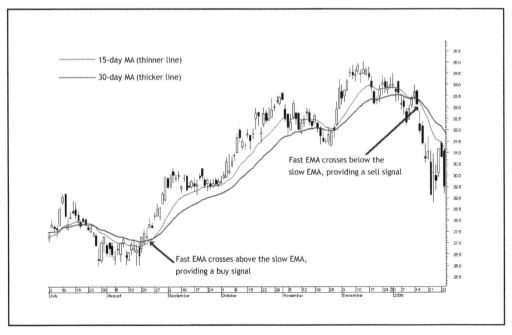

Basically, the longer the period of time of the MAs chosen, the more significant the crossing signals will be. A crossing of a 15-week and 30-week MA is far more important than the crossing of a 15-day and 30-day MA. The longer the timeframe, the less they cross, making it a stronger signal when they do. Shorter timeframe moving averages are more likely to cross regularly.

11

MACD histogram

The MACD histogram is a momentum indicator that is produced from the MACD indicator. This indicator is used to confirm the strength of the trend and give warning of possible changes.

In order to understand how the histogram works, it is important to know how the MACD indicator works.

MACD

MACD stands for 'moving average convergence/divergence'. It is a trend-following indicator that provides signals similar to two moving averages, because it is produced based on a calculation of a series of moving averages. It appears as two lines on a chart—a solid line and a dashed line. Their purpose is detailed below.

- The solid line is calculated by subtracting a 12-day exponential moving average (EMA) from a 26-day EMA of the share price and is then plotted on the chart.

- The dashed line is based on a nine-day EMA of the solid line.

The crossovers of these two lines provide buy and sell signals for short-term traders:

- Buy signals are generated when the solid line crosses above the dashed line.

- Sell signals are generated when the solid line crosses below the dashed line.

So it's the same signals that two moving averages generate. Figure 11.1 shows how the MACD appears on a chart and how it works.

Figure 11.1: daily chart with MACD indicator

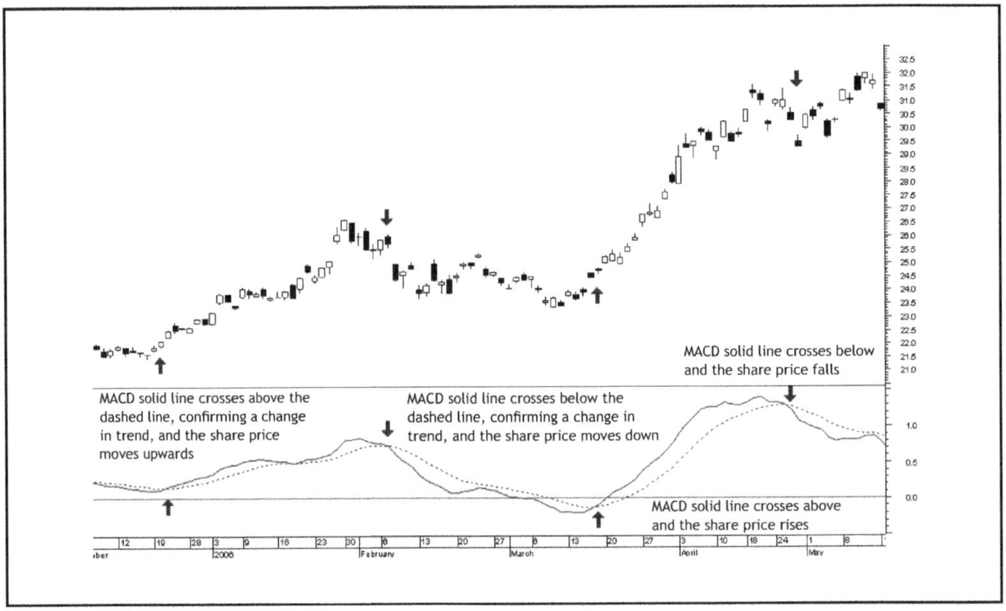

MACD histogram

The histogram provides a deeper insight into the trend of a share than the MACD. It confirms the strength of the trend and any signs of possible weakness when it diverges from the trend. It is produced based on the actual movements of the MACD indicator.

How the MACD histogram works

The MACD histogram oscillates above and below a zero line into positive and negative territory. It is calculated by taking the difference between the two MACD lines and plotting this to form a histogram.

The movements of the MACD indicator are reflected in the histogram in the following ways:

- If the MACD solid line is above the dashed line, the MACD histogram will be positive and plotted above the zero line.

- If the MACD solid line is below the dashed line, the histogram will be negative and plotted below the zero line.

- When the two lines of the MACD touch, the histogram equals zero.

The histogram then increases and decreases in size, in either negative or positive territory, as the spread between the two MACD lines changes. When the spread between the MACD solid line and dashed line increases, the histogram will rise in size, becoming taller or deeper (depending on its direction). When the two MACD lines draw closer together, the histogram becomes shorter in size.

Figure 11.2 shows how the histogram appears on the chart of a share and how it moves above and below the zero line.

Figure 11.2: daily chart with MACD histogram

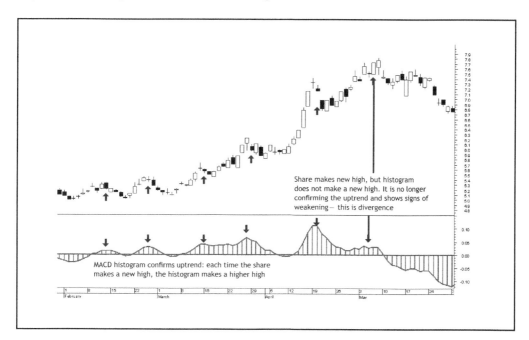

Trend confirmation

The histogram basically tracks market sentiment and can provide a hint of what lies ahead. New highs or lows in the histogram are usually followed by new highs or lows in the share price.

If the histogram rises to new highs during an uptrend, making a new higher peak as the share makes a new high, this confirms the uptrend is healthy. In this situation, you can expect the next price rally to retest or possibly exceed its previous high.

If the histogram falls to new lows during a downtrend, this confirms the downtrend will continue and you are likely to see the share price retest or possibly exceed its previous low.

Divergence

Divergence signals are an early warning sign of a possible change or weakening in the share price. Divergence occurs when the price and the histogram move in opposite directions. It is usually most obvious and significant at market tops or bottoms.

There are two types of divergence: bearish divergence and bullish divergence.

Bearish divergence

Bearish divergence occurs above the zero line on the positive side of the histogram. In an uptrend, prices make many new highs and the histogram confirms the trend by making new higher peaks above the zero line, mirroring the share price. Bearish divergence occurs when the market makes a new high and the histogram fails to reach a higher peak than its last. This contradiction indicates that a divergence is present, which suggests a weakening trend. You can see bearish divergence in figure 11.2 (on page 103).

Bullish divergence

The opposite is true in a downtrend, so bullish divergence occurs below the zero line. In a downtrend, prices make many new lows and the histogram confirms this by making lower peaks below the zero line. If the share price makes a new low and the histogram does not also make a new low, bullish divergence is evident. This suggests a weakening of the downtrend.

Failed signals

It's important to understand that no indicator is 100 per cent accurate—signals can fail. I would estimate that divergence is effective 60 to 70 per cent of the time and for the remaining 30 per cent, the share price will not react to it. Divergence is only indicative of sentiment, which can change extremely quickly. Figure 11.3 is an example of failed divergence in the histogram where the share continued to rise.

If you identify divergence in a chart and the share fails to react to this and does not follow through, this is a failed signal and shows that the share is very strong. As with any failed technical analysis signal, this is an extremely powerful signal in itself.

Figure 11.3: daily chart with a failed divergence signal

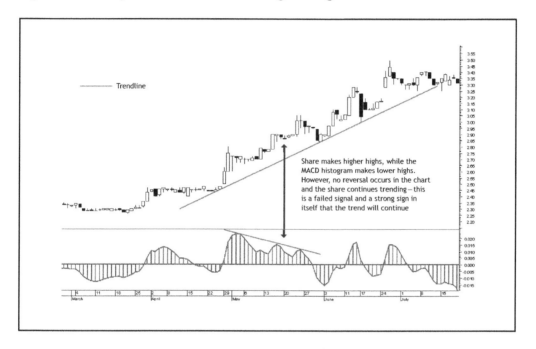

12

Average true range

The average true range (ATR) is a volatility indicator that tells you the average price movement of a particular share in one day or over a set period. If you apply it to a daily chart, it gives you a value of the average share movement (either up or down) in one day. I use this indicator to understand the share's current volatility and to assist me in setting my stop losses.

How the ATR is calculated

The ATR indicator is calculated by taking the greatest of the following ranges and averaging it out over a set number of periods:

- the difference between the current high and current low price

- the difference between yesterday's closing price and the current high price

- the difference between yesterday's closing price and the current low price.

The default setting for the ATR is 14 periods. This means that it takes the greatest of the ranges listed above for the last 14 trading days (for a daily chart) and then averages them out to give a value that indicates how much (on average) that particular share can move up or down in a day.

ATR and volatility

The ATR assists traders in understanding the volatility of a share and how much movement it is capable of in one day. The best way to think of the ATR value is as a percentage of its share price. The average daily movement of a share compared to its price determines how volatile the share is. For example, if a share is priced at $10.00 and its current ATR value is $0.30, this share can move, on average, 3 per cent in one day either way. If another stock is priced at $10.00 and has an ATR of $0.65, this share could move, on average, 6.5 per cent in one day either way. Obviously, the second stock is much more volatile than the first one and you would want to buy fewer shares to allow for a larger price movement.

Applying the ATR

To calculate the current ATR value of a share, technical traders simply apply the ATR indicator to the chart, as shown in figure 12.1. The last value plotted is the current ATR for the share.

Figure 12.1: daily chart with an ATR plotted

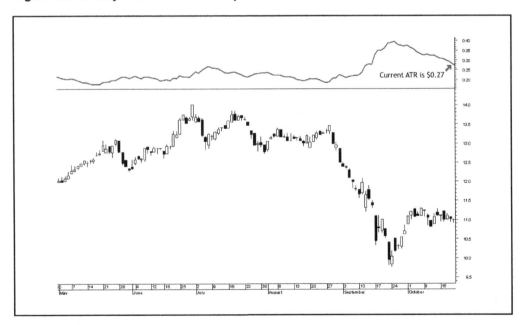

As you can see, the ATR indicator moves up and down and changes over time as the share price activity changes. These movements indicate the changing activity of the share price. So if the ATR is at a higher price than previously, then the share has increased in volatility. If it is at a lower value than previously, then the share price is fairly constant.

ATR and stop losses

Because the ATR is a measure of volatility, many traders use it to assist in setting a stop loss (stop losses are covered in detail in chapter 15). To do this you simply take a multiple of the ATR value from the entry price—this may be two or three times the ATR value.

For example, if you were using a multiple of 3 ATR to set your stop loss and the share you are buying is trading at $11.00 and has an ATR of $0.27, then you would set your stop 3 times $0.27 away from the share price—that is, $10.19 ($11.00 – $0.81). This ensures that the share's current personality is taken into account. All shares are different and will have varying volatility at different times.

The ATR multiple a trader selects to set a stop loss will depend on his or her trading style. The larger the multiple, the further away the stop loss is from the share price. A multiple of 2 ATR would be a much tighter stop loss and you would not hold the share for as long because you are not giving the share as much room to move. This would suit a short-term trader. A medium-term trader would want to give the share more room to move in order to hold the trade open longer. A medium-term trader is more likely to use a multiple of 3 ATR or more.

The ATR value can also be used on weekly charts to provide the average weekly movement of the share price. Long-term investors may use a multiple of a weekly ATR value, because this provides a much wider stop than a daily ATR.

13

Volume

Volume measures the total number of shares that change hands each trading day. It is usually plotted as a histogram at the bottom of a share chart (as shown in figure 13.1). The height of each line tells you the number of shares that were traded for the day—the longer the line, the more shares changed hands that day.

Volume helps define the share's liquidity and the strength behind the current movement. I personally use volume for these reasons and also to confirm breakouts from trading ranges.

Figure 13.1: daily chart with volume

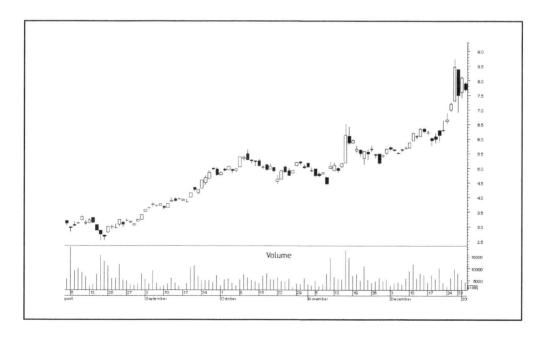

Liquidity

Volume is also referred to as liquidity—how liquid a share is. Liquid stocks have strong demand, meaning there are a lot of buyers and sellers available at each price level and they have high volume each day, making it easier to buy and sell a share. Illiquid shares lack demand and have only a few buyers or sellers available, making the shares harder to buy or sell at the price you want.

Liquidity is important in selecting shares to buy. I believe it is best to own stocks that you can easily enter and exit with a readily available supply of buyers and sellers in the market. All blue chip stocks trade in the millions per day, while small speculative stocks may only trade a few thousand a day. I personally prefer to trade within the top 300 stocks of the Australian market to ensure that there is always sufficient liquidity available on the share.

Volume and trends

Volume helps measure the intensity of price movement. It is a major factor behind the commitment of the buyers and the sellers in the market and helps to confirm trends.

For a price increase to be sustained, it must be fed by new buyers. When a share is healthy and in an uptrend, this is supported when volume increases as the price rises and decreases as the price falls. This confirms that the upward move has strength and that the share is likely to continue trending higher. This is a general rule, however, and cannot be applied to every price movement.

Figure 13.2 is an example of a share in an existing long-term uptrend. It demonstrates how volume can play an important role when the share price rises with the longer term trend and then decreases on counter trends.

Volume and breakouts

So while volume helps to measure the level of intensity of a price move and confirm the trend, it is also very important when it comes to breakout signals for entry. When a share consolidates sideways, buyers and sellers are in equilibrium so volume tends to decrease during this time. Volume usually picks up before prices rise and then increases sharply when it breaks out of its trading range, giving an entry signal and showing that buyers are behind the new move.

Figure 13.3 shows the classic volume pattern that occurs when the share consolidates and then breaks resistance above its trading range.

Figure 13.2: daily chart showing volume confirmation of the trend

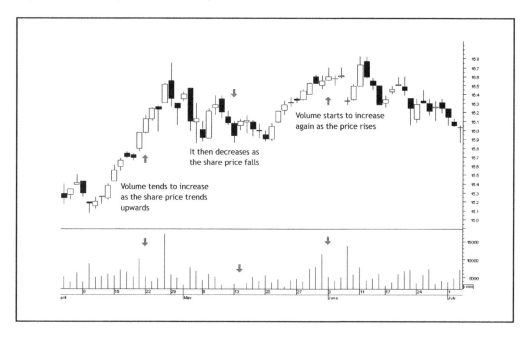

Figure 13.3: weekly chart showing volume increase on the breakout

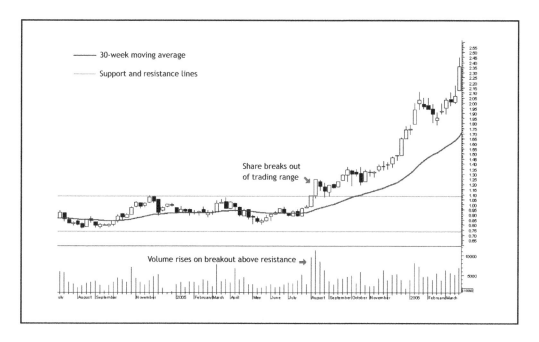

Part V Trading plan: risk management

14

Risk and money management

Stop!

Red light!

Do NOT start trading until you have read this section.

Risk and money management are the most critical parts of your trading plan. Even if you get everything else in your plan wrong, you are on the right path to success if you adhere to strict money management rules. You may not believe it, but this is the honest truth. Most people think trading is all making great entries and picking the right share. I'm sorry to say this is not so.

Even systems with random entries are still profitable as long as they have good money management rules and follow the golden rule of trading—let your profits run and cut your losses short. In his book *Trade Your Way to Financial Freedom*, Van Tharp discusses random entries and demonstrates that you can make money consistently with a coin flip system, as long as you have a good exit strategy and size your positions based on minimum risk—which is what this part of the book is all about.

How to manage your risk in the market

Your long-term success as a trader depends on how you manage your risk in the market. Unfortunately, you can't control the market—you don't know what's going to happen tomorrow or the next day—but you can control your risk management.

This is what has enabled me to survive during the tough times and prosper in the good times.

In the end, it does not matter how many winning trades you have in your portfolio. If you can't keep your profitable trades larger than your losses, you will not survive in the market — it only takes hanging on to one or two bad trades in your portfolio in the hope that they will get better again. Yet some stocks, like One.Tel and HIH, never recover.

The key to controlling risk in the market is to use simple money management techniques to protect your trading capital. Ask yourself the following questions:

- *How much risk are you prepared to take on each trade?* Position sizing is a money management tool you can use to control risk. It will help you determine how many shares you can buy based on the percentage risk that you are prepared to undertake on any one trade.

- *What is the maximum position size you will take on any one position?* Successful traders understand the need to spread their risk in the market and ensure that no single position exceeds a set percentage of their total capital.

- *How will you manage your total open market risk?* Portfolio heat is a method used to manage your overall risk in the market at any one time. If all your trades were to hit their stops tomorrow, you already know your worst-case loss.

- *How will you limit your losses and protect your open profits in a trade?* Stop losses are your key to survival when entering a trade and allow you to protect your open profits once the trade moves your way.

Your trading plan should cover all this information. To start with, consider how much capital you can dedicate to trading and how you plan to allocate this to the market.

Total capital

How much capital can you devote to trading? You may decide to start out with a small amount and build it up as your confidence increases. However much capital you have, this is the value that you will use to position size your trades and determine how many shares you can buy.

Capital allocation

How do you plan to allocate your capital to the stock market? Determine how you will divide your capital between your different trading systems and different parts of the market.

For example, if you were trading both a long-term system and a short-term system, how will you split your capital between the two systems? Will you allocate 50 per cent to each system or favour one over the other?

Do you plan to trade a range of different markets or instruments? Some traders like to invest the majority of their capital in the most liquid part of the market and put less money into the less liquid part of the market. Will you put 100 per cent of your capital into the S&P/ASX 100 stocks? Or do you want to invest in the entire market? You may decide to allocate a higher percentage of your capital to the S&P/ASX 100 stocks and a lower percentage to other areas of the market.

Different shares have different market capitalisation (which affects their liquidity) and this determines which indices they belong to. The way to work out the market capitalisation of a stock is to take the total number of shares on issue and multiply this by its average share price. The higher capitalised stocks belong to the S&P/ASX 100 followed by the top 200, 300 and so on. The S&P/ASX 100 are considered to be the lowest risk stocks on the market, the bottom 200 of the S&P/ASX 300 are medium risk and anything outside the S&P/ASX 300 is considered higher risk and more speculative. You can find out more about which shares belong to which index by visiting the ASX website <www.asx.com.au>.

Total number of positions

How many open trades can you comfortably manage at once? This is an individual decision that will change as you gain confidence in the market.

You may be comfortable juggling five shares or perhaps you can handle having 10 trades active at any one time. It's all about understanding your comfort zone. If you find you can't sleep at night, or if you are feeling stressed about your trading, then you most likely have too many positions open and it's time to scale down.

Position sizing

Position sizing basically answers the question of how many stocks you can buy. It is a key part of your money management strategy that is designed to manage risk.

There are a few different methods that you can use to position size in the market —the main two are the equal portions model and the percentage risk model.

Equal portions model

The equal portions model is a very simple method used by many beginner traders. It involves dividing your trading capital into a certain number of equal amounts and then purchasing shares based on these amounts. For example, let's say you have $50 000 available to trade. This model involves splitting your equity into, say, five equal portions, so that you can open five share positions worth $10 000 each.

For example, if you want to open a position in ABC shares that is trading at $3.20, this means you can buy 3125 shares ($10 000 divided by $3.20). If the second position you want to open is with XYZ shares, trading at $16.00, this means that you can buy 625 shares.

This method is simple and easy to work out and ensures you keep all your positions equal in size across your portfolio. However, the equal portion model assumes that all trades are equal in risk and does not take into account whether or not the share is highly volatile. For example, buying $10 000 worth of BHP Billiton shares is very different to buying $10 000 worth of a highly speculative mining stock that is still digging for gold.

Percentage risk model

You may have heard of the '2 per cent rule'—a lot of professional traders talk about it and this is what the term 'percentage risk model' refers to. Percentage risk is a methodology that ensures you never lose more than a set percentage of your trading equity on any one trade. Traders use this to determine their position sizes.

For example, if you have $50 000 available to trade, you may be prepared to risk 2 per cent of this on any one trade. This means that you are prepared to risk a maximum of $1000 on any one trade. This does *not* mean that you purchase $1000 worth of any one share. Rather, it is the dollar value you are comfortable losing on a trade.

The things you need to know in order to position size based on this model include:

* your total capital

- the percentage of your capital that you are prepared to risk on any one trade—this may be 2 per cent, 1 per cent or 0.5 per cent
- where your initial stop loss will be set
- the entry price at which you will purchase the share.

To better understand how this method of position sizing works, let's take a look at an example.

Let's say you receive a trading signal on ABC share and decide to buy. You have a trading account of $50 000 and you have decided to risk 2 per cent of this on any one trade. ABC share is currently trading at $2.14 and your chart shows a support level at $2.00. You decide to set your initial stop loss below the support level at $1.98. This means that you will exit the trade if the share falls $0.16 in value to $1.98.

Because $1.98 is your initial stop and worst-case loss, you will use this to determine how many shares you can buy.

Total capital	=	$50 000
Risk % allocation	=	2%
Risk $ allocation	=	**$1000 ($50 000 × 2%)**
Entry price	=	$2.14
Stop loss	=	$1.98
Risk value	=	**$0.16 ($2.14 – $1.98)**

Based on this information, position sizing involves dividing your 'risk $ allocation' by the 'risk value' (the difference between the stop loss and the buy price).

Position size	=	$1000 ÷ 0.16
	=	6250 shares can be purchased
Total trade size	=	6250 x $2.14 (entry price)
	=	$13 375 (excluding brokerage)

If ABC share falls in price by $0.16 to $1.98, then you would exit the trade taking a loss of $1000—which is 2 per cent of your trading capital.

This model means that you know your risk upfront and must exit if the share hits your stop loss. No matter how many positions you take in the market, your risk will always be limited to a small fixed percentage of your available capital. This limits your potential downside and protects your trading capital.

Maximum position size

You must also set a rule in your trading plan as to the maximum position size you will take out on any one trade. This ensures that you diversify your money in the market and spread your risk. Most professional traders ensure that no single position exceeds 25 per cent of their capital when they size their trades.

Set yourself an additional rule when position sizing to ensure that the total position you open does not exceed 25 per cent of your capital. If it does, then you must purchase fewer shares. The larger the portfolio you have, the lower the maximum percentage position size you can allocate. For portfolios in the hundreds of thousands, it might be a good idea to drop your maximum position size back to, say, 20 per cent or 15 per cent.

Let's take a look at the ABC share example again. With a capital base of $50 000, no position should exceed $12 500 in total or 25 per cent. The total trade size in this example is as follows:

Position size	=	$1000 ÷ 0.16
	=	6250 shares can be purchased
Total trade size	=	6250 x $2.14
	=	$13 375 (excluding brokerage)

Obviously, this size exceeds 25 per cent. With your total position never exceeding $12 500, you could only buy the following number of shares:

Total investment < 25%	=	$12 500
Share price	=	$2.14
Total number of shares	=	$12 500 ÷ $2.14
	=	5841 shares

This may seem like a lot to work out when sizing a trade and it does take practice to begin with. To make it easier I have developed a *Position Sizing Calculator* in the form of an Excel spreadsheet. As a special bonus, you can download it for free by visiting <www.smarttrading.com.au> and clicking on the 'Free book bonuses' link.

Portfolio heat

Portfolio heat basically answers the question of how many new positions you can have open at any one time. Professional traders use this technique to manage and quantify their total risk in the market. They understand that trading is about the successful management of risk and they always know what the worst-case loss would be if all their positions were to hit their stops today.

For example, if you always position size your trades based on risking 1 per cent of your total capital, how many of these trades would you be prepared to have open at any one time? In dollar terms, how much money would you be willing to lose if all your stops were hit in one day? By answering these questions, you will be able to determine a suitable portfolio heat level.

Let's say that you risk 1 per cent of your capital on each new trade and you are willing to withstand a 5 per cent portfolio heat level. This means that you have no more than five initial positions open at any one time. So your worst-case risk if all your stops were hit tomorrow would be 5 per cent of your total equity (excluding brokerage costs).

When you have opened up five initial positions in the market at a total of 5 per cent risk, you cannot open up any further positions until one of the trades moves in your favour and you are able to move your initial stop loss to breakeven. Once you have moved an initial stop to breakeven, this means that your portfolio heat now drops back to 4 per cent and you can open up a new position at 1 per cent risk (if one becomes available and you still have trading capital available). More information on setting and moving stop losses is covered in the next chapter.

If you are using 2 per cent risk, then you may decide to set your portfolio heat to 6 per cent. This means you can have three initial positions open at 2 per cent risk each.

When starting out as a trader, it is best to keep your portfolio heat set at a low level. Once you have two or three positions open, wait until you have moved one of the initial stop losses on a trade to breakeven before opening another. This will help you manage your risk in the market while you are still learning.

Conclusion

By being proactive and incorporating money management strategies into your trading plan, you now have the opportunity to improve your returns in the market.

At first you will make a lot of mistakes and it is money management that will enable you to survive and ensure that you continue to trade, even after a cluster of losses (which is inevitable with trading). Limit your risk in the market by position sizing all your trades based on a set percentage of risk, diversifying in the market by ensuring no position exceeds 25 per cent of your capital and managing your total open market risk through a set portfolio heat level.

Figure 14.1 shows a sample money management statement from a trading plan to guide you in preparing your own money management strategy.

Figure 14.1: sample statement from a trading plan for a beginner long-term investor

Money management

Initially, I will allocate myself a trading account of $50 000 to trade up to a total of six positions. I will:

- allocate this capital to S&P/ASX 300 stocks only

- position size my trades based on 2 per cent risk ($1000)

- ensure no single position exceeds 25 per cent ($12 500)

- manage a portfolio heat level of 6 per cent.

Once I have gained enough confidence with my trading I will add another $50 000 to my trading account and then reassess my risk levels.

✔ *Smart action step*

Sit down with your calculator and work out your risk management strategy. Decide how much capital you will dedicate to trading, how you plan to allocate it to the market, how many positions you feel you can comfortably handle having open at one time and how you plan to size those positions and manage your total open market risk.

Don't forget to visit <www.smarttrading.com.au> to download your free *Position Sizing Calculator*, if you haven't done so already.

15

Stop losses

Novice traders often spend too much time on entries and trying to pick the right share. It is how you manage the trade after you enter it and how you exit it that will determine if it is successful or not. This involves using stop losses.

What are stop losses?

Stop losses are a capital preservation tool that traders use to exit trades when they move against them. The goal of a stop loss is to protect your capital by keeping your losses small and protecting your profits once a trade moves your way. I never enter a trade without first setting a stop loss. When a trade moves favourably, this stop is raised and continues to be raised until eventually the share hits my stop and I exit the trade.

Different types of stops

To take the emotions out of trading and to ensure that you limit your losses and protect your capital, it is best to use a range of stop losses. You will need to set an initial stop loss before you open a trade. As the trade progresses, this will be moved to a breakeven stop to protect your capital and then to a trailing profit stop to protect your profits as the trade continues to move your way.

Initial stop loss

The initial stop is your most critical stop and is a vital step to take before opening a trade. This is your worst-case stop that will limit your losses on a trade and preserve your capital. Use initial stops to position size your trades and determine the number of shares you can buy based on your set risk.

Although this stop will produce a loss if it is hit, it limits the size of the loss and protects you from taking a severe loss if the trade you open is not successful. Your goal as a trader is to exit the trades that fail and stay with the ones that continue your way.

The initial stop can be set based on a range of methods, including the following:

- *Per cent retracement*—this is based on a set percentage fall in the share price. As an example, let's use 10 per cent as the percentage fall. If you were to buy a share at $10.00 and it falls by 10 per cent (or $1.00), you would exit. Your initial stop loss would be set at $9.00 ($10.00 – $1.00). You would then position size your trade based on this stop loss. Be aware that this type of stop assumes all trades are equal.

- *Trendline*—this stop is all about staying with the long-term trend of the share and is used by technical traders. It involves identifying the trend of the share and the important support levels on the chart of the share (covered in chapter 3) and setting your initial stop loss below one of these levels with the goal of exiting if the share falls below it.

- *Technical indicator*—this type of exit involves using a technical indicator, such as the trend indicators listed in chapter 9. You would set your stop loss below the indicator. For example, if you were to use a moving average indicator over the share price, you would set your initial stop loss below the moving average value line with the goal of exiting if the share falls below it.

- *Volatility*—this involves taking the volatility of the share into account. The best way to do this is to use a volatility indicator and take a multiple of this value. For example, if you were to use the average true range indicator, then you would take, say, three times this value off your buy price and this would be where you set your initial stop loss.

Breakeven stop

A breakeven stop allows you to lock in a no-loss trade. It is the price level at which you bought the stock (give or take brokerage costs). As the share moves your way, you want to raise your initial stop to this level. This stop now protects your capital and ensures you do not lose any money if the share fails to continue to rise.

The initial stop loss should be moved to a breakeven stop after a certain movement has occurred in the stock. The share may have made a series of new highs from your entry, or it may have risen by your per cent retracement amount (for example, 10 per cent) or a multiple of the average true range you set as your initial stop loss.

Trailing profit stop

This stop results in exiting a trade with a profit. When a share is trending strongly in your favour, move your breakeven stop to a trailing profit stop and continue to raise this as the share continues to move favourably. Your goal is now transformed from protecting your trading capital to protecting your profits.

You need to use a method to identify when you would exit and take your profits. These stops can be set and managed using methods similar to those used to set the initial stop loss:

- *Per cent profit retracement*—an example of this would be to set a 10 per cent retracement as your initial stop loss and carry this through as the share moves your way. Each time the share rises in value by 10 per cent, set your stop loss 10 per cent below this level. Basically, you trail a 10 per cent stop underneath the share price as it moves favourably. If the share falls by 10 per cent in value, you exit and take your profits.

- *Trendline*—this involves trailing your stop loss underneath the trendline of a share, identified by viewing the share's chart. Once the share breaks below its trendline, you exit and take your profits. This is illustrated in figure 15.1 (overleaf).

- *Technical indicator*—this could be a break below a trend indicator, such as a moving average or the crossover of two moving averages. If your entry method was based on a cross of the fast-moving average above the slow-moving average, then you may exit when the fast-moving average crosses below the slow-moving average. This is illustrated in figure 10.4 on page 98.

- *Volatility*—take a multiple of a volatility indicator (such as the average true range) and trail this underneath the share price. Once the share falls by a multiple of this amount, you simply exit.

Figure 15.1: trendline stop example

The numbers identify areas where you can set your stop loss under the trendline as the trade progresses

Exit when share breaks trendline

Other types of stops to consider

In addition to the initial, breakeven and trailing stop losses, you may consider incorporating the following types of stops into your exit strategy.

Time stop

The time stop involves setting a limit on the length of time you will stay in a trade if the share does not move as expected. This ensures that you don't tie your money up in a trade that is going nowhere and enables you to move it into another opportunity. It is all about making your money work hard for you.

The difficulty is in setting the time stop. How long should you leave your money in a share that is going nowhere before you exit? There will be times when you exit a trade only to watch the share take off in your favour. One of the best ways to set this stop is to look at your average hold time in the market (covered in chapter 21), take a third of this and use it as your time stop. For example, if you hold a trade for 30 days on average then you would use 10 days as your time stop. Alternatively, you could look at past trades and determine how long on average they took to move to breakeven and use this as a guide for your time stop.

Profit stop

A profit stop involves setting a profit target and exiting the trade once it achieves this level. This may be based on percentage gains or a set price target. It is often used to capture windfall profits when a share rises by a large amount in a short space of time and is different from the usual price activity of the share.

It is difficult to decide when to exit and take profits. Some traders undertake a partial exit approach, where they exit part of their position as the share rises by set amounts. For example, when the share rises 10 per cent in value, they exit one-third of their position. When it rises another 10 per cent in value they exit another third of their position and then exit the final third when it rises 10 per cent in value again. Other traders may use a method where they tighten their stop loss as the trade continues their way until it is eventually hit. These methods are common among short- to medium-term traders. Long-term traders usually don't set profit targets and tend to stay with the trade until their trailing profit stop is hit.

Although it makes sense to take profits as the trade moves in your favour, it goes against the golden rule of trading—let your profits run. Profit stops can actually limit your profits, because you are pulling money out of the trade as the share moves your way. Successful traders build a position by adding to the trade by set amounts as it moves upwards. This strategy is called pyramiding and is covered in chapter 19.

In the end it comes down to what you are most comfortable doing. If you feel more comfortable undertaking a staged exit approach and taking partial profits along the way, make sure you understand its disadvantages and be aware that it can reduce your performance in the market.

Psychological stop

Psychological exits are all about knowing yourself. If you are the type of person who can cause damage to your trading account during certain events in your life, then you need to employ psychological exits.

These events include travelling, feeling ill or burnt out, feeling stressed, moving house, having a baby and so on. These are the times when your probability of losing money in the market is greater because you are unable to act on your plan and trade unemotionally in the market. You should not open any new positions in the market during these times and you may consider employing a psychological exit to close out your existing positions.

Another time to consider making a psychological exit is when you are on a losing streak. It can be stressful trying to play catch up and you can let your emotions override your trading plan. Consider taking a break from the market and then re-enter with a conservative approach by using a lower risk level, not entering as many trades and staying out of high-risk shares.

Setting stop losses

There are two ways that a trader can set stop losses in the market: automatically or manually.

An automatic stop is a stop-loss instruction set with your broker either online or over the phone. If the share falls to or below this price level your trade will automatically be exited.

A manual stop is a stop you set mentally and you keep track of. If at any time the share falls to or below this price level you need to take action and exit the trade. These stops require careful monitoring and discipline to act on them when they are hit. I used to act on my stops using this method when I first started trading, before automatic stops were available. Now, with automatic stops, I don't have to worry—I know my stop loss will be actioned for me and there is no need for me to keep track of the markets each day.

Be aware that whichever method you choose, there are no guarantees that you will exit at your exact price and you may have to exit at a lower price if the share never trades at the set price level. For example, a share may gap and open at a lower price than your stop when the market opens, or there may be insufficient demand at the price level you set. This is called slippage and is part of the cost of trading. Guaranteed stop loss orders (GSLOs) traded through CFDs are an exception to this rule—they are covered in chapter 8 as one of the advantages of CFD trading.

Why are stops so important?

You cannot control the markets or determine how far a stock will fall and when it will happen. The only thing you can control is how you manage your risk in the market. If you set a stop loss, you must follow it. Figure 15.2 is an example of how a situation can rapidly get worse if you don't have the discipline to exit when a share breaks its trendline.

If you have trouble exiting based on a stop, I suggest you make a copy of figure 15.2 and put it on your wall as a reminder of what can happen if you don't follow your exit signal. Being aware of the danger of a large loss like this will reinforce the importance of acting on stops and help you become a better trader. It only takes one trade like this to wipe out your entire profits for the year or possibly more.

Figure 15.2: Centro Properties (weekly chart)

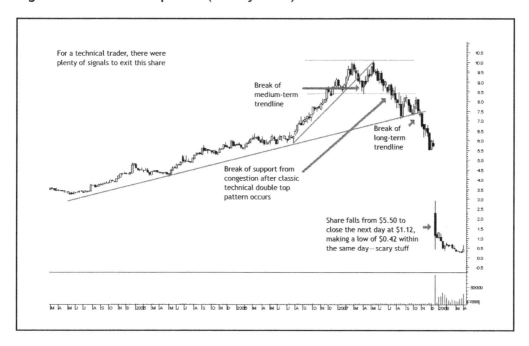

Stop losses are the key to your success

Position sizing your trades by using an initial stop loss on a set percentage of your capital will ensure you limit your losses. Then, as the share goes your way, a trailing profit stop strategy will allow you to protect your capital and then protect your profits.

Once you select a method that suits you, stick to it. Trading is all about consistency and following a set of rules—this will ensure your survival in the market and enable you to make profits. It's very easy to buy a share, but exiting the share is the most challenging part. This is the difference between successful traders and those who fail — successful traders know that the secret to their success is in the exits.

✔ *Smart action step*

Determine how you will set your stop loss for the different stages of a trade. Think about how you will set your initial stop, when you will move this to a breakeven stop and then eventually a trailing profit stop. This information will be documented in your trading plan in the next section, under *System Development*.

16

Market exposure guidelines

Trading can be frustrating. Even if you carefully pre-plan everything that you do, there will come a time when you hit a cluster of losses or the markets turn sour. How will you cope during these times? Will you lessen your exposure? Will you change your strategy? These are the questions you need to ask yourself when completing this section of your trading plan.

Remember, *you* are the most important part of your trading. Make sure you think about how you will handle trading during difficult times in your life.

Series of losses

When you open a trade, one of two things will happen—it will either be profitable or unprofitable. As discussed in previous chapters, not every trade is going to be profitable, so it's important that you understand that losses are an inevitable part of trading. The traders who fail are the ones who cannot control their losses.

Throughout your trading career you are bound to experience a run of losses and you need to consider what you will do in this situation. You will become very emotional when it first happens and you may self-sabotage if you continue to trade through a losing streak. You may think the stock market owes you and undertake strategies such as doubling your bet size to win back big—but you may just dig yourself into a bigger hole by doing so. Ask yourself:

- How will you handle a cluster of losses?

- At what point will you stop trading?

- Do you plan to take some time out to re-evaluate your trading and review your psychology?

- Will you tone back your exposure in the market? This can be done by halving your position size and slowly re-entering the market when you are ready.

The majority of professional traders usually have a 50 per cent reliability, which means that only half of their trades will be winners. But they know that the secret lies in keeping their wins large in size and cutting their losses short to keep them small. I know that I keep repeating this golden rule, but it is important that you understand it. I neglected to follow it in my early days of trading and acted like a know-it-all teenager. The market soon showed me the light and it did not take me long to realise that I needed to follow this rule in order to be profitable.

In the end, it will only be a few trades a year that will make you the big money. Your goal is to break even and protect your capital on the other trades and avoid risks that will put you out of the business of trading.

Time-out strategy

This is where your psychological exit comes into force. You need a time-out strategy to cope when other events in your life make trading difficult. Consider the following:

- What will you do with your trades when you go away on holidays?

- What if you move house, move interstate or overseas?

- What if you or someone in your family becomes unwell and is suddenly taken to hospital?

- Do you have someone who knows your trading positions and can act on your behalf? Or do you have an online system with automatic stop losses set to protect your trading capital?

When things are happening in your life or family, you can't focus on trading; make a plan as to what you are going to do in these situations. Take a step back — the market is not going away; it will still be open when things get better again.

Your plan might be to take a break from trading altogether. Or, if you trade a long-term and a short-term system, turn off your short-term system and focus on your long-term system only. Once things settle down, begin trading the short-term system again.

Market trends

The two main market trends are bull and bear markets. A bull market is the most favourable market to trade and the one that most people know how to trade. However, markets also trend down and these markets are called bear markets. What will you do when the markets change and a bear market hits? What level of exposure will you have in the market during this time?

Bull markets

During a bull market, share prices across the entire market generally increase. To profit in a bull market, traders simply buy shares and hold them for the long term, riding the uptrend until it ends. These markets produce large returns for long-term investors. What we don't know is how long a bull market will last. History has shown that bull markets are usually slow and steady and can trend upwards for many years.

Trading a bull market is also known as going 'long'. So when you own a share, you have a long position in that share. Your view on the share is usually bullish and it is purchased with the goal of selling at a higher price in the future. This is where the profits are made.

Bear markets

Share prices across the entire market generally fall during a bear market. These markets can be fast and furious and are usually shorter in duration than a bull market, wiping out a lot of profits and turning profitable trades into losses very quickly. It is impossible to predict how low prices will fall — once the panic hits, fear spreads very quickly and drives prices down fast.

Trading a bear market is also known as going 'short'. This is when you have a bearish view on a share. Basically, you sell a share that you do not own with the goal of buying it back at a lower price in the future. Aim to trade short if you want to profit in a bear market, or sit on the sidelines and wait it out until favourable market conditions re-emerge.

A bear market is usually the hardest market to trade because short selling is not a common strategy in Australia. Yet it is a strategy that professional traders undertake to profit during a bear market. You can short sell through derivative instruments (by purchasing put options or put warrants), through shares or CFDs.

What is short selling?

Short selling is similar to buying a share, only the buying and selling order is reversed. Instead of buying a share and then selling it, you actually sell the share first and then buy it back at a later date.

How to short sell shares

To short sell shares you need to use a broker that offers this facility. The broker actually borrows the shares from somebody who owns them (possibly a large institutional investor) and you sell them in the market to open a short trade. For example, let's say you want to short sell 5000 XYZ shares. You will actually borrow those 5000 XYZ shares and sell them in the market. You sell them with the expectation that the share will fall in price and you will buy it back at a lower price when you exit the trade. The shares will then be given back to their original owner.

In effect, you are actually borrowing shares that you do not own and your broker organises this for you. You usually have to pay a borrowing fee to do this and put up some money for margin.

Your profit or loss is the difference between your sell price and your buy price. So if you exit at a lower price than you opened the trade, you will make a profit. If the share increases and you exit at a higher price than you entered, you will incur a loss.

In the Australian market you can usually only short sell the top 200 shares. The ASX keeps track of all short positions in the market each day. All brokers must report their net short-sold positions to the ASX each trading day and this data is collated into a short-sold position report. You can find out more about short selling and view this report by visiting the ASX website—search for 'short selling' for more information.

Dividend implications

Be aware that when you short sell there are dividend implications. You will be required to pay out the dividend (plus possibly franking credits) if the share goes ex-dividend while you have a short position open. This is because the original owner of the share will want to receive their dividend and franking credits. You have only borrowed their shares to short sell and they still have the rights to the dividend and any franking credits.

Ensure you are always aware of the upcoming dividends for shares when you are short selling. If a share is due to pay a dividend in the next few days, you may consider holding back on the trade and short sell it after this occurs.

There is, however, one benefit when a share does go ex-dividend—if the share is in a downtrend (which it should be if you are planning on short selling it), it can drive more momentum into the fall and cause it to fall further.

So, how will you handle a bear market?

You have two choices and simply hanging on in hope is not one of these—well, not for me anyway! You can:

- Act on stop losses for long trades and keep out of the market until conditions become favourable again. This is a strategy that long-term investors are most likely to use.

- Act on stop losses for long trades and start short selling—professional traders use this strategy because their goal is to be profitable in all kinds of markets.

Prepare yourself for a bear market and pre-plan how you will handle it.

Summary

It is your money management rules that will enable you to survive in all kinds of markets. When you hit a cluster of losses, you will survive with a small drawdown if you have position sized your trades with a small percentage of your equity and you are managing your maximum portfolio heat in the markets. Consider taking a step back to reassess your trading and the current market conditions during difficult times.

Figure 16.1 (overleaf) provides a sample statement from a trading plan to guide you in preparing your own market exposure plan.

Figure 16.1: sample statement from a trading plan for a long-term investor

Market exposure

During a cluster of losses I will take some time out and reassess things. I will re-enter the market when I feel ready by halving my position size and increase it when I am confident enough to do so.

I will also lessen my exposure in the market when I go away on holidays or if I can't focus on trading during difficult times in my life.

I am a long-term trader and will only trade long in the market. During bear markets I will follow my stop-loss strategy and exit trades as my stops are hit. I will sit out of the market until I see it becoming healthy again and then I will re-enter and slowly build positions back into the market.

✔ Smart action step

Determine your level of exposure in the market when you hit a cluster of losses, what your time-out strategy will be during stressful or distracting events in your life and how you will handle a bear market.

Part VI  Trading plan: system development

17

The trading system

You are now armed with all the information you need to start developing your own personal trading system. You have decided on your trading style, the instrument(s) you plan to trade and the indicators you plan to use. Now you can put all this information together and start developing your trading system(s).

The system might be a mechanical trading system, which means that you turn your entry rules into a scan and use software to scan the market searching for opportunities. This is what I do with MetaStock. MetaStock has an Explorer function that I can code with my entry criteria and search across a selection of shares for those that meet my trading rules. Now is your chance to develop your trading rules and put it all together to go into your trading plan.

To start with you need to consider what the objective of your trading system is, what market you will trade the system with and what direction the system will trade.

The objective

What is the objective of this trading system? What sort of trades are you looking for? Is this a short-term, mid-term or long-term system?

Below are some examples of objectives for a range of different trading systems. As you can see, they are all very different and this will give you some guidelines to assist you in putting together an objective for your own trading system.

- *Long-term investor using fundamental analysis*
  The objective is to search for growth shares with low P/E ratios that show potential for further growth and will provide an income stream through regular dividend repayments.

- *Medium-term trader who is trading swing moves*
  The objective is to trade a swing move in a share that is already trending. This involves identifying shares that are in an existing trend and waiting for a retracement opportunity when the share moves back to its trendline and bounces.

- *Short-term day trader*
  The objective is to capitalise on intraday price swings by concentrating on four selected stocks each day that have good liquidity and volatility.

Market selection

What instrument will you trade with this system? What market or section of the market will be used to trade this system? Below are some examples of different instruments that different styles of traders may select:

- A long-term investor would most likely concentrate on shares only, because there are no time limits and they will receive the advantage of dividends and franking credits. They may limit themselves to the top 300 or the entire market and focus only on those stocks that have a good dividend yield.

- A medium-term trader who trades swing movements may use derivative instruments (such as options or warrants) and purchase one with an expiry date within the usual trading timeframe. Alternately, he or she may trade the individual share or CFD, focusing on the S&P/ASX 100 or 300, and run a scan searching for trades each day.

- A short-term day trader may decide to trade a derivative instrument such as CFDs because they usually involve lower brokerage costs and lower capital due to the margin. This makes it cheaper to do a large number of trades. A short-term trader will most likely concentrate on a small selection of stocks using intraday charts, focusing on the most liquid stocks to ensure ease of entry and exit with a good price movement in order to profit. This may involve selecting from the top 10 stocks of the market or just concentrating on the top shares of a particular sector, such as the banking sector. Another option is to trade the index itself, such as the S&P/ASX 200 or other CFD instruments like foreign exchange or commodities.

Market direction

A long-term investor who is focused on building a portfolio of shares will most likely focus only on trading long. Medium- to short-term traders want to profit in all kinds of markets, so they are more likely to trade both long and short.

Figure 17.1 is a sample statement that a long-term technical trader may include in this section of their trading plan.

Figure 17.1: sample statement from a trading plan for a long-term technical investor

---

The trading system

Objective:

Build a long-term portfolio of shares by searching the market for shares in an existing uptrend and stay with this long-term trend until signs appear that the trend is changing.

Market selection:

S&P/ASX 300 stocks only.

Market direction:

Long only.

✔ Smart action step

Now is the time for you to have some fun and start developing your trading system. Based on the style of trading that you have selected, determine the objective of your trading system. What markets will you run this system over and which direction will it trade? Document this information in your trading plan.

18

The entry

Defining your entries is the fun part of developing your trade rules. The best way to get started is to consider what type of share it is that you want to own. This can be broken down by defining the ideal set-up criteria that must be present in a share for you to consider it to be a good buy and what trigger you are looking for to enter the trade.

Just imagine that you are going on a long car journey. You usually set the car up to ensure that it is right before you leave. You either get it serviced or look it over yourself by checking the oil, battery fluid, tyre pressure and ensuring you have enough petrol to get you to the next service station. Once you are happy that the car is ready for the long journey, you can finish packing and get ready to go. You turn on the car and drive automatically, which is what you want to do with trading. Once the set-up conditions are present in a share and you see a trigger, you want to pull that trigger and place the trade. You want to be able to do this unemotionally and this is achieved by following your trading rules.

Your goal is to take the guesswork out of your trading and have a clear set of rules to trade the market in an unemotional and disciplined way. Let's get started and put these rules together.

Ideal set-up criteria

What conditions must be present before you would consider adding a share to your watchlist?

For a technical trader this is all about identifying shares that are healthy. Ask yourself: 'What conditions must be present in the chart of the share that confirms it is in an uptrend?' You may use some of the indicators that you selected at the end of chapter 9. Here are some sample trading rules that a technical trader may use to identify an uptrending share:

- share price is rising and making a series of higher highs and higher lows

- an uptrend line can be drawn on the chart

- there is no immediate overhead resistance

- the long-term moving average is rising and the share price is trending above it

- the fast moving average has crossed above the slow moving average

- more up days are occurring than down days (if you are using candlestick charts this would mean that more white candles are present than black candles in the chart)

- momentum indicator confirms the trend and is making new highs as the share price rises to new highs

- volume increases as the share price moves upwards, supporting the upward movements

- the share is liquid with good average volume and is in the S&P/ASX 300.

Figure 18.1 is a sample chart displaying some of these trading rules and it meets the ideal set-up criteria of a healthy uptrending share. It is a good idea to take the time to look at charts of shares you would like to have owned and ask yourself what set-up was present in these charts. This will help you to formulate your ideal set-up criteria.

For a fundamental trader, the set-up criteria will be based around the company's financial results. These results may help to identify good-value companies that have the potential for future growth. Ask yourself: 'What financial statistics have to be met for me to consider adding the share to my watchlist?' An example of these statistics might be:

- share has a P/E ratio less than 20

- the dividend yield is greater than 4 per cent

- share is liquid and belongs to the S&P/ASX 300.

Figure 18.1: an uptrending share (weekly chart)

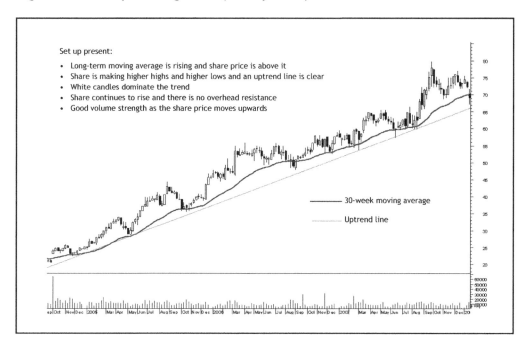

Set up present:

- Long-term moving average is rising and share price is above it
- Share is making higher highs and higher lows and an uptrend line is clear
- White candles dominate the trend
- Share continues to rise and there is no overhead resistance
- Good volume strength as the share price moves upwards

30-week moving average

Uptrend line

Triggers for entry

Once you have defined the set-up that must be present to add a share to your watchlist, you now need to define what will trigger you to enter a trade. You may have a selection of shares that meet your ideal set-up criteria and you need to choose from this selection. So how will you do this?

A fundamental trader would simply select the shares with higher dividend yields from his or her watchlist, especially if a regular income stream is important for the portfolio.

A technical trader, on the other hand, will look for a trigger on the daily chart of the share, such as a share breaking upwards to a new high or a retracement trigger of a share pulling back to its trendline (or support line) and bouncing. Figure 18.2 (overleaf) shows a chart with the ideal set-up criteria present and identifies these two types of triggers that could be used to enter a position in an uptrending share.

Figure 18.2: example of entry triggers (daily chart)

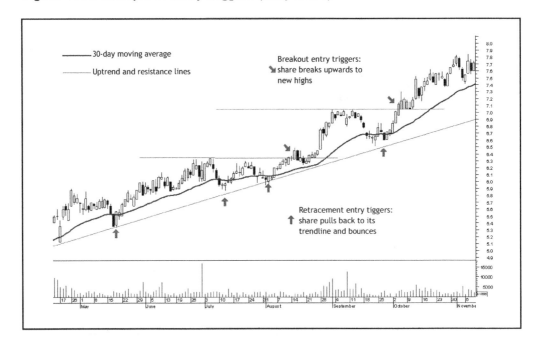

Placing the order

Once a share meets your ideal set-up criteria and you receive a trigger to enter, it is time to pull that trigger and place the trade. How will you place an order in the market?

Firstly you need to decide how many shares you can buy. I covered position sizing in chapter 14 and discussed the two methods you can use—either equal portions or percentage risk. Personally, I use the percentage risk method and examine the chart of a share to determine where to set my initial stop loss and size the trade accordingly.

Once I know how many shares I can buy, I will either buy that day (if the market is still open) or the next day if the market is closed. I prefer to buy once the market has settled down—when the market opens at 10 am it is very volatile. Extreme price movements occur because the market has to process the mad rush of orders placed as the market opens. I don't like to get caught up in the adrenalin rush at the open and prefer to wait until the market settles before placing my order, usually half-an-hour to an hour after the open.

Once I am ready to place my order, I check the market depth. Figure 18.3 shows an example of a market depth screen for National Australia Bank, provided by Commsec. Most online brokers offer market depth to their customers free of charge. The market depth provides details of the current share price and shows the queue of buyers and sellers that have placed bids and offers in the market for the share. When a match occurs between the buyers and sellers, a sale is made. This is shown as the 'Last' traded price and the market depth is adjusted accordingly.

Figure 18.3: example of market depth

▲ NATIONAL AUST. BANK FPO ▲

Code	Bid	Offer	Last	Change*	% Change*	Open	High	Low	Volume
NAB	34.940	34.950	34.950	+0.350	1.01	35.150	35.260	34.650	495,801

Buy | Sell | Add to Watchlist

Market Depth

	BUY			SELL		
Number	Quantity	Price	#	Price	Quantity	Number
1	136	34.940	1	34.950	1,780	2
4	19,374	34.900	2	34.970	6,000	1
1	34	34.880	3	34.980	7,054	1
1	34	34.870	4	35.000	8,972	3
1	4,060	34.850	5	35.030	1,500	1
1	2,000	34.810	6	35.080	11,775	1
1	399	34.790	7	35.130	3,161	1
1	247	34.750	8	35.150	4,000	3
1	2,000	34.710	9	35.170	1,000	1
1	3,958	34.700	10	35.200	17,653	4
	837 buyers for 459,321 units				611 sellers for 595,894 units	

© Commonwealth Securities

I use the market depth to help time my entry into a trade. If I view the depth and I am happy with the price at which the share is trading, I will place my order. If I feel the share price has run away and moved significantly, I will keep my eye on it—if it settles back down I will then place my order.

When placing an order in the market you have a choice of buying at the current market price or setting a limit price. I place most of my orders at market so that my trade goes through immediately. I can't be bothered playing around for a couple of cents difference. If I want in, I simply get in. The only time I would hold back is if I feel the share has run away, as I mentioned above.

At-market orders

To make an at-market order, you place an order to buy a share at the current available market price, which is the current offer price from the next available seller. Your order is filled automatically as soon as it is placed. These orders can only be placed during market hours and when the share is trading, meaning it has not been halted or suspended from trading. At times, shares will go into trading halt due to the impending release of an announcement. Once the announcement is released, they will commence trading again. Only limit orders can be set outside market hours or when a share is halted.

At-limit orders

To make an at-limit order, you set a price at which you want to buy the share. Your order will sit in the queue of the market depth until it moves to the top of the queue and is matched out by a seller willing to sell at your requested price. There are no guarantees that your order will be filled and it may sit in the market until you cancel it. Your broker may automatically cancel it at the end of the trading day if it is not filled. Different brokers offer different ways to set limit orders. Some only give you one option, others give you two. The most common at-limit orders are 'good for the day', which means the order is only active for one day and cancelled if not filled. 'Good till cancelled' means the order will remain active until it is filled or you cancel the order. You will only be charged brokerage once the order is filled.

Figure 18.4 shows a sample statement from a trading plan to demonstrate how you would include your entry rules in your trading plan.

Figure 18.4: example statement from a trading plan for a long-term investor

The entry

Ideal set-up criteria:

Share is healthy and the chart shows:

- it is in an uptrend with no immediate overhead resistance

- it is trending above its long-term moving average

- it has a rising momentum indicator

- there is increasing volume supporting the trend.

Trigger for entry:

Share is breaking through to new highs or retracing and bouncing off its trendline.

Placing the order:

I will place my orders 'at market' after the market has settled.

✔ Smart action step

Take the time now to study some healthy shares and work out the ideal moment to enter these shares. Write down the ideal set-up conditions that were present and the best entry points. This determines your trigger to buy. Doing so will help you to develop your personal trading rules and document them in your trading plan.

19

Trade management and the exit

Choosing the share is just the beginning—the most important and challenging part of the trade comes next. It is how you manage and exit the trade that makes it successful and determines if you will be profitable in the market over the long term.

Even if the trade is a profitable one, there is still a danger of cutting the profit potential if it is not managed effectively. That is why it is so important to have a clear stop-loss management plan and exit when your stop is hit in order to minimise the losses and protect your open profits. Spend time developing this as part of your trading system rules and ensure you are comfortable with them. Most importantly, ensure that you adhere to them.

It's just like driving a car. There is a set of rules you need to follow in order to arrive at your destination safely. You need to stop at traffic lights when they turn red, you need to give way to your right at intersections, you need to abide by the speed signs along the way and you must not drink and drive. These rules have been set for your own safety and the safety of others. Yes, you may break some of them from time to time, but you will bear the consequences if you are caught.

Trading is no different. Your exit rules are there to protect you and your capital. You may get away with breaking these rules from time to time, but if you get caught out and don't exit a trade when you should have, you may suffer the consequences. Remember figure 15.2 on page 133—you would have lost a lot of money if you did not follow your exit rules in this trade.

Setting your stop losses

I covered stop losses in chapter 15 and discussed the different types and how to set them. You may have already considered how you will set your stops after reading this chapter. If not, please review chapter 15 again to assist you in developing your trade management rules.

To ensure that you cover all areas of your trade management, ask yourself:

- How will you set your initial stop loss?

- When will you move your initial stop loss to breakeven?

- When will you move your breakeven stop to a trailing profit stop and start protecting your profits?

- How will you manage your trailing profit stop?

- Will you use a time stop? If you will, how much time will you give the share to move if it does not move favourably after entry and your initial stop loss is not hit?

- What would you class as a windfall profit and how will you handle this?

Exit criteria

What conditions need to occur to make you exit a position or warn you to watch or tighten your stops? You need to develop a clear set of rules as to when things become unfavourable and what action you will take. This might be to exit the trade, tighten up your stop loss closer to the share price or sell half the trade and continue to hold the remainder until your stop is hit.

Previously, you defined the key criteria that must be present in a healthy share and these formed your trading rules for entry into a stock. Next, let's define the key criteria that indicate a share is becoming unhealthy. For a technical trader this means the share is now trending down and is not the sort of share that you would want to own. Simply reverse the criteria for a healthy share. For example:

- share price is falling and no longer making higher highs—it is now making a series of lower lows and lower highs

- share breaks below its uptrend line, signalling a possible end of its healthy trend

- a downtrend line is evident on the chart of the share

- the share is breaking through support levels

- the share is trending below its long-term moving average and this indicator is falling

- the fast moving average has crossed below the slow moving average

- more down days are occurring than up days (if you are using candlestick charts this would mean that more black candles are present than white candles in the chart).

Figure 19.1 is an example of a chart that displays some of these exit criteria and is showing signs of becoming unhealthy.

Figure 19.1: example of exit criteria showing in a chart (weekly chart)

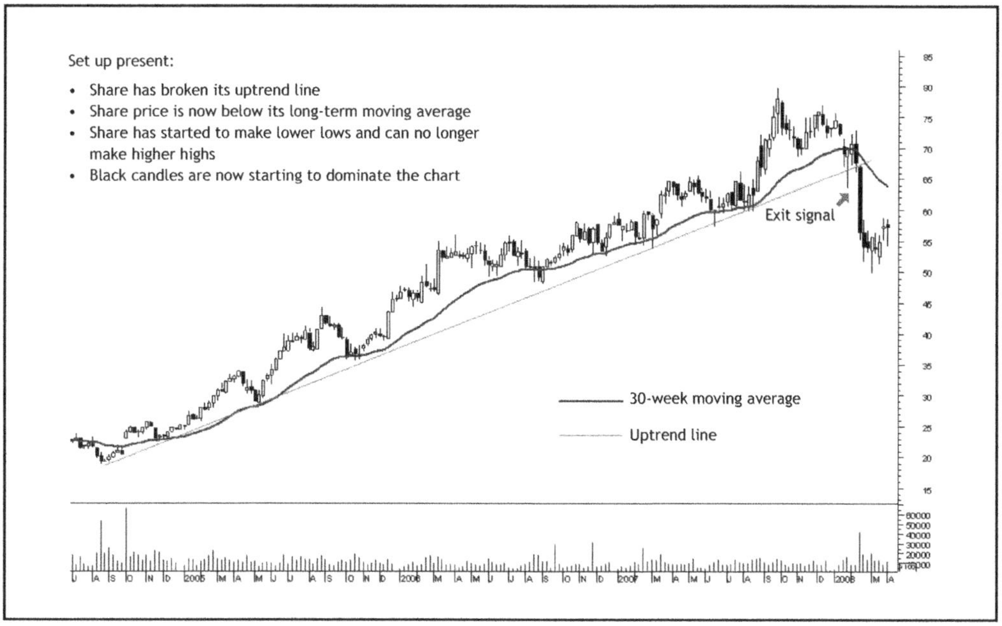

This list of rules that you develop will provide you with clear guidelines when things are becoming unfavourable. Ask yourself what you plan to do if any of these conditions occur.

Exiting the trade

Actually exiting your trades can be difficult to do. You can either monitor them manually and exit by placing a sell order in the market when the share falls to your stop loss, or you can set an automatic stop loss so you will be automatically sold out of the trade if the share trades at your stop level or below. I covered these methods in chapter 15. What method will you use?

Some people like to have control over exiting and prefer to do it themselves, while others like it to happen automatically. There is no right or wrong.

If you have trouble exiting and pulling the trigger when your stop is hit, or you procrastinate and second-guess yourself, I recommend you use an automatic stop facility. These days most brokers offer automatic stops. I love them and use them for all my trades. It takes less of my time to monitor my trades and makes trade management so much easier, especially as I have two young children at home. There are often times when things are happening and I can't check the market that day. When this occurs I know that this is not a problem because I have automatic stops set and everything will be taken care of for me. I simply set an automatic stop each time I open a trade at my initial stop and leave it set until such time as the share moves favourably and I get a signal to move my stop upwards. I then amend the stop order to the new price. This can be set any time during or after market hours.

Pyramiding

Professional traders use a technique called pyramiding to build positions and add to an already profitable trade. If you have a winning trade, ask yourself:

- Will you add more money to the position?
- If so, at what stage will you do this?
- How will you size the additional entries?
- What stop-loss techniques will you implement on the additional entries?

The most effective way to pyramid is to purchase more shares in smaller lots than the first trade. As the trend unfolds and the share moves in your favour, add to the share by buying smaller parcels each time. That is why this money management strategy is called pyramiding—you build a position based on the largest parcel first and then each additional parcel is smaller than the previous, as shown in figure 19.2.

Figure 19.2: pyramiding illustration

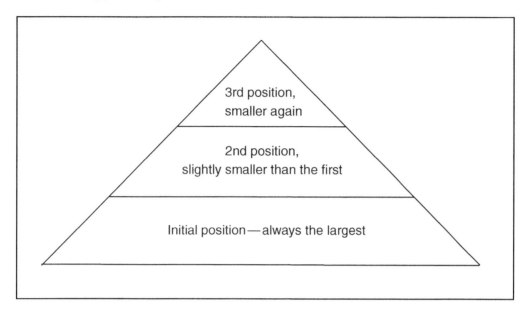

So if you were using the percentage risk method (as discussed in chapter 14) you would pyramid into a share using a decreasing percentage of risk each time. Let's say that you always open your first trade based on risking 2 per cent of your capital. When you add to the trade you would size the position on a smaller percentage of risk each time. For example, your second position could be based on 1 per cent risk and the third based on 0.5 per cent risk. Alternatively, if you are risking 1 per cent on the first trade, then risk 0.5 per cent on the second and 0.25 per cent on the third. You are simply halving your risk each time you add to the position and sizing the new trade based on this risk level. This will ensure that your first entry is always your largest.

When to pyramid

Set milestones to help you determine when to act and pyramid into a trade based on your risk levels. Some traders like to pyramid and buy more once the stop loss on their initial trade has moved to breakeven. For example, if they size their first trade based on 2 per cent risk, once their stop moves to breakeven they have locked in a no-loss trade. They now risk 1 per cent of their equity and buy more. This means they will only take a 1 per cent loss if their stop loss is hit.

Other traders, like myself, prefer to pyramid once a trailing profit stop is active and will risk some of these profits to buy more. Let's look at an example.

Let's say you have an account of $50 000 and you have decided to risk 2 per cent of this on any one trade. You purchase a share and position size the trade based on risking $1000. You buy the share at $2.00 and decide that if it falls by 10 per cent you will exit the trade. Therefore, your initial stop loss will be set at $1.80 ($2.00 minus $0.20). In summary:

- The initial position is entered based on a 10 per cent drop in the share price and sized according to 2 per cent of your trading capital.

- Once the share rises above your entry price by 10 per cent, move your stop to breakeven. You have now locked in a no-loss trade.

- Once the share moves another 10 per cent (or 20 per cent from your entry price) your stop loss will move to a trailing profit stop. You are now protecting a profit of $1000, which was your original risk value on the trade. You could now consider adding more money to this trade and buy more shares risking 1 per cent ($500) of your capital. This means that you are now risking half of your open profits from the initial trade, so if the share does not continue your way and your trailing profit stop is hit after you pyramid you will still profit by $500.

- You can continue to pyramid in increments like this. If the share rises a further 10 per cent (30 per cent from your entry price) you could buy more, risking 0.5 per cent this time, and so on.

Trade management strategy

Spend time developing your exit strategy and ensure that you are comfortable with it. It is important that you adhere to your strategy and take action when a stop is hit.

Figure 19.3 shows an example trading plan statement for a long-term investor to assist you in documenting your own trade management rules.

Figure 19.3: sample statement from a trading plan for a long-term investor

Trade management strategy

Stop losses:

- The initial stop loss will be set either below the trendline or below a significant support level.

- Once the trade is in profit by the initial risk the stop loss will be moved to a breakeven stop—which is the buy price.

- The trendline will then be used as the trailing profit stop and I will exit if this breaks anytime.

- A time stop will be set for a three-month period. This means if my stop loss has not moved to a breakeven stop within three months I will consider exiting.

- If at any stage the share becomes volatile and starts rising a large amount in a short space of time, I will sell half and take windfall profits.

- I will set automatic stop losses in the market and change these as required, so I will be automatically exited out of the trade when the share hits my stop.

Pyramiding:

Once my stop loss has moved to a trailing profit stop, I will keep my eye on the share and consider purchasing more if another entry trigger is provided. I will size the trade based on half the risk of the initial position. The new trade will then be managed the same as the initial position.

✔ Smart action step

Study a range of old charts showing healthy uptrends and ask yourself when would have been a good time to exit these shares. What conditions were present in these shares when the uptrend ended? Use this information and the stop-loss rules that you developed from the action step in chapter 15 to determine your exit strategy.

20

Trading routine

As part of your trading strategy development, you need to decide when you are going to undertake all your trading activities. We all have set routines in our daily lives. You get up in the morning, have a shower, have breakfast, clean your teeth and so on. Without realising it, you are doing the same thing every morning and sticking to a routine. Trading is no different and having a trading routine is critical to ensuring success.

Develop a routine plan that lists the activities you plan to do day to day, week to week and so on. These activities would include reviewing the market activity, searching for opportunities, placing trades, monitoring existing positions and evaluating your trading performance. These key activities are all covered in this book and must be a part of your routine if you want to maximise your trading potential.

These activities will vary depending on what type of trader you are and will be undertaken at different times to suit your style and the amount of time you have available for trading. For example, a short-term trader will undertake a lot of activities on a daily basis, whereas a long-term trader will not necessarily have a daily routine and is more likely to focus on weekly, monthly or annual routines.

Don't worry if you do not know what your trading routine will be yet — it will develop over time. To help you get started, let's review the activities that you may undertake as part of your trading routine.

Reviewing the market activity

As a trader it is important to get a feel for what is happening in the market place, both in Australia and overseas. Below are some activities that you may undertake to do this. These activities will be different for technical and fundamental traders—technical traders will use charts to view this information, while fundamental traders will use company information and will be more interested in news-related activities.

- Check the international markets each day to determine what to expect in the local market. If there is a big change in the US markets in particular, there tends to be a reaction in the local market when it opens. Short- to medium-term traders would check international markets each day, but long-term traders would not necessarily be interested in doing so. They have a much longer term view and are not so interested in the day-to-day activities of the markets.

- Review international and local finance news. Depending on your trading style, this may be a daily or a weekly activity.

- Undertake a world market review by scanning the charts of the major global and Australian indices to determine the current market trends. This activity would be best done on a weekly or monthly basis so that you can see the changes in trend over a period of time. Figure 20.1 is a chart of the All Ords to show you how you can view an index chart in MetaStock.

Figure 20.1: weekly chart of the All Ords index

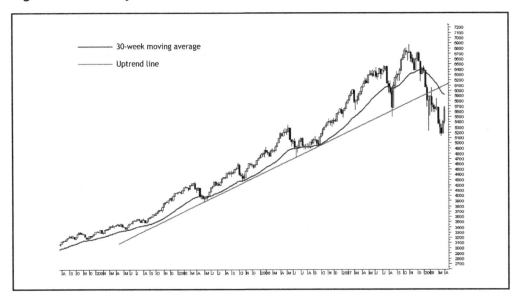

- Review the charts of the major Australian sector indices and use their trends to determine which sectors are healthy and which are unhealthy. The market is made up of 12 Globally Standardised Industry Classifications (or GICs). They include sectors such as Financials, Energy, Utilities, Telecommunication and Industrials. Like the world market review, this activity is best done on a weekly or monthly basis. Figure 20.2 is a chart of the Financials sector to show you how you can view sector charts in MetaStock.

Figure 20.2: weekly chart of the S&P/ASX 200 Financials Index

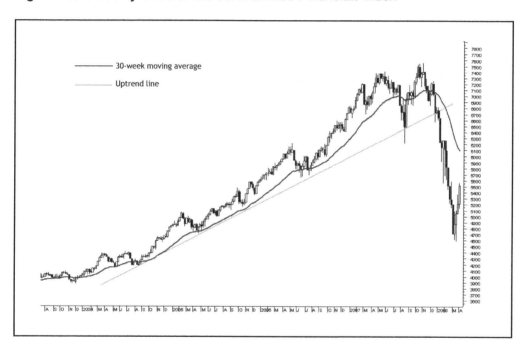

Reviewing the market may take an hour or two, but you can spread this task over a week. Some activities are best undertaken daily while others should be undertaken weekly, as previously indicated.

Searching for trades

Once you have reviewed the markets and feel that it is a good time to enter new trades, start searching for opportunities and creating a watch list. If you are a technical trader you will use charts to do this. You may do it manually by viewing all the charts of a specific index (such as the S&P/ASX 100) or sector (such as the Financials sector) and adding promising charts to a watchlist. Or, if you have the software to do so, you may run an automatic market scan to search for shares that meet your entry criteria.

Fundamental traders often use software that provides company statistics and enables them to run market scans searching for key criteria, such as P/E ratios and dividend yields above or below a certain amount. Or they may just focus on a set index of shares (such as the S&P/ASX 100) or a healthy sector of the market and research these companies.

Some of the activities involved in searching for trading candidates include:

- *Scanning the market for possible trading candidates.* As I mentioned previously, MetaStock has a function called the Explorer and I have it coded with my entry criteria. To run a scan, I simply select the trading system I want to run from the Explorer list (as shown in figure 20.3), press the 'Explore' button and away it goes. It runs my scan across a selected custom folder of shares (such as the S&P/ASX 300) and produces a report of all the shares that meet my exploration rules. Figure 20.4 shows how MetaStock runs the scan and when it is complete the report appears, as shown in figure 20.5.

Figure 20.3: MetaStock Explorer function

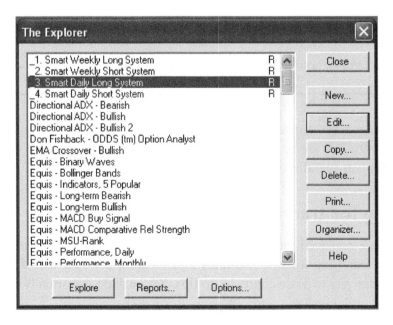

Figure 20.4: MetaStock Explorer running a market scan

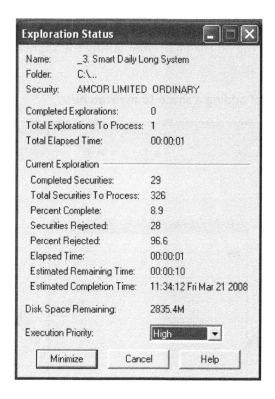

Figure 20.5: MetaStock Explorer market scan report

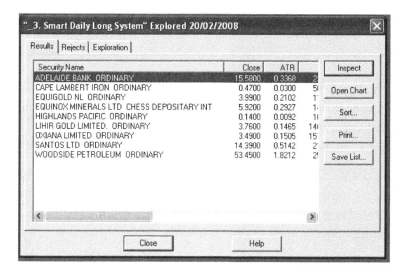

- *Creating a watchlist of shares.* In MetaStock, this simply involves opening all the charts from the Explorer report and examining each one. If any shares match my ideal set-up criteria, I add them to my watchlist folder. This involves right-clicking on the chart and adding the share to 'My Favourites', as shown in figure 20.6.

Figure 20.6: example of adding a share to my watchlist

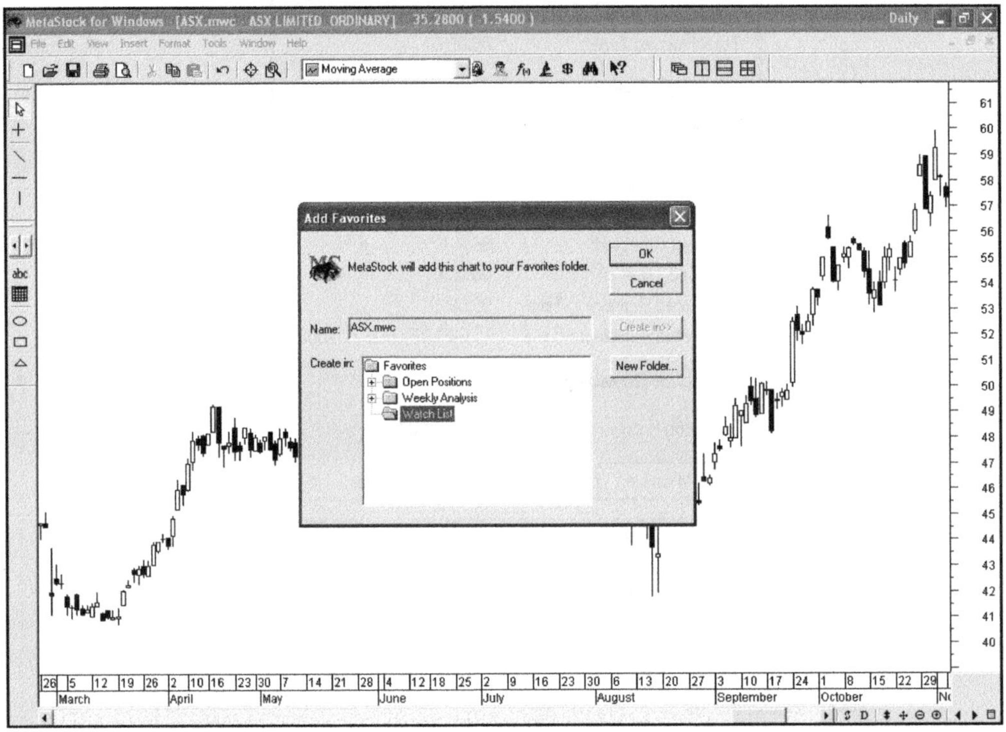

- *Selecting trading candidates.* This involves reviewing the shares in my watchlist folder. If a trigger presents itself, it's time to take action and place a trade. I will calculate how many shares I can buy and then place a trade with my broker and set an automatic stop loss.

- *Regularly cleaning out your watchlist folder.* Either make a habit of deleting any stocks that no longer fulfill your set-up criteria as you browse through your watchlist searching for triggers or make it a regular routine to clean out your watchlist folder once a week or once a month.

The time required to do these activities will vary anywhere from 10 minutes per day to many hours per week. If you are a technical trader who uses charting software to run a market scan, it shouldn't take long to create a watchlist and review this list for trading candidates. For a fundamental trader this could take a lot longer, because it takes time to review company information and statistics.

Managing trades

Once you open a trade you will undertake regular activities to manage it. These activities are usually done on a daily basis if you are a short- to medium-term trader and on a weekly basis for long-term traders. They will take approximately 15 to 20 minutes to complete and they include:

* Review open trades to see if any action needs to be taken, such as moving stop losses, exiting a trade or buying more stock. For me, this involves opening the charts of my trades and examining them. When I enter a trade in the market I add the chart to a folder I have created called 'Open Positions' in my Favourites folder in MetaStock. Then all I need to do is open this folder, scan through each of the charts and raise my stop loss if any of the shares have moved favourably. The different methods you can use to set stop losses are covered in chapter 15.

* Update your records with any changes you have made to your portfolio, such as opening new positions, updating stop losses and other actions to be aware of. Consider keeping a trading diary or using a portfolio management spreadsheet or software to manage your records. I discuss the importance of record keeping in chapter 21.

  I use a product called the *Smart Trader Spreadsheet* to track and manage all my trading activity. This can be purchased from <www.smarttrading.com.au>. It includes a range of worksheets that allow me to track, manage and understand what is happening in my portfolio at any point in time. When I open a new trade, I set up a new worksheet dedicated to that trade and document all the information on the trade and manage it until it is closed. Figure 20.7 (overleaf) shows an example of a trade worksheet. It tracks a range of detailed information for each trade—entry details of the trade, stop-loss tracking, exit information, dividend details and diary entries to document reasons for entry, exit and feelings throughout the trade.

Figure 20.7: sample trade worksheet from the *Smart Trader Spreadsheet*

ALL

Portfolio

Currency of Trade	AUD
System Category	1
Risk %	1.00%
Margin	90.0%
Total Reduced Equity	$110,704

Initial Purchase

	AUD	AUD
Date		19-Mar-04
Exchange Rate	$1.0000	
ATR	$0.2602	$0.2602
ATR %	8.5%	8.5%
Buy Price	$3.060	$3.060
Brokerage	$20.00	$20.00
Other Fees	$35.45	$35.45
Risk %	1.00%	1.00%
Risk Premium	$1,107.04	$1,107.04
Initial ATR Stop	3.0	3.0
Initial Stop	$2.279	$2.279
Quantity	1,418	1,418
No. Purchased	1,290	1,290
Total Trade Value	$4,002.85	$4,002.85
Capital Outlay	$450.19	$450.19

Stop Loss AUD

	Signal	Actual Stop
Current Price	$9.650	$12,948.85
Highest Close or HHV	$9.960	$10,132.85
Current ATR	$0.5300	
Quantity	1,290	
Initial Stop		$2.279
Breakeven Stop		$3.118
Chandelier Stop	3.0	$8.370
Panic Stop	2.0	$8.590
Current Stop Loss		$8.370

Initial Sale

	AUD	AUD
Date		
Exchange Rate	$1.0000	
Sale Price		$0.000
Brokerage	$0.00	
Other Fees	$0.00	
Quantity		0
Total Sale	$0.00	$0.00
Profit / Loss	$0.00	$0.00
% Return (on total trade value)		0.00%

Trade Monitor

	AUD	AUD
Exchange Rate	$1.0000	
Open Quantity	2,200	2,200
Current Stop Loss	$8.370	$8.370
Current Price	$9.650	$9.650
Highest Close or HHV	$9.960	$9.960
Open Value (as per stop)	$18,394.00	$18,394.00
Total Trade Buy Value	$8,561.15	$8,561.15
Total Capital Outlay	$942.02	$942.02
Trade Sale Value	$0.00	$0.00
Profit / Loss	$10,132.85	$10,132.85
% Return (on capital outlay)	1075.65%	1075.65%

Summary

Trading Instrument			CFD
Total Hold Time (days)			364
Trade Profit / Loss			$10,132.85
Trade Direction			Long
Time Stop (optional)		42	30-Apr-04

Pyramid 2

		AUD	AUD
Date			4-Jun-04
Exchange Rate		$1.0000	
ATR		$0.3100	$0.3100
Entry Trigger	6.0	$4.920	$4.920
Actual Buy Price		$4.710	$4.710
Brokerage		$20.00	$20.00
Risk % GSLO	0.00%	$0.00	$0.00
Risk % Capital	0.50%	$553.52	$553.52
Total Risk Premium		$553.52	$553.52
Initial ATR Stop		3.0	3.0
Initial Stop		$3.780	$3.780
Quantity		595	595
No. Purchased		640	640
Total Trade Value		$3,034.40	$3,034.40
Capital Outlay		$321.44	$321.44

Stop Loss AUD

	Signal	Actual Stop
Highest Close or HHV	$9.960	
Current ATR	$0.5300	
Quantity	640	
Initial Stop		$3.780
Breakeven Stop		$4.773
Chandelier Stop	3.0	$8.370
Current Stop Loss		$8.370

Sale 2

	AUD	AUD
Date		-
Exchange Rate	$1.0000	
Sale Price		$0.000
Brokerage	$0.00	
Other Fees	$0.00	
Quantity		0
Total Sale	$0.00	$0.00
Profit / Loss	$0.00	$0.00
% Return (on total trade value)		0.00%

Open Risk Monitor

	AUD	AUD
Capital Insured by GSLO		$10,797.30
Protected GSLO Profit		$2,536.15
Trade $ Risk		$0.00
% Risk		0.0%
Profit / Loss as per Stop		$10,132.85
Open Profit / Loss		$12,948.85
Average Buy Price	$3.8914	$3.8914

Total Trade Size

	AUD
Maximum % Trade Size	20%
Maximum $ Trade Size	$22,140.83
Trade Approved	Yes
Maximum Quantity Allowed	2,712

LONG TRADE

Details

Company	Aristocrat Leisure
Sector	Industrial
Broker	
Other Info	

Pyramid 3

		AUD	AUD
Date			20-Aug-04
Exchange Rate		$1.0000	
ATR		$0.3100	$0.3100
Entry Trigger	9.0	$5.850	$5.850
Actual Buy Price		$5.570	$5.570
Brokerage		$20.00	$20.00
Risk % GSLO	0.00%	$0.00	$0.00
Risk % Capital	0.25%	$276.76	$276.76
Total Risk Premium		$276.76	$276.76
Initial ATR Stop		3.0	3.0
Initial Stop		$4.640	$4.640
Quantity		298	298
No. Purchased		270	270
Total Trade Value		$1,523.90	$1,523.90
Capital Outlay		$170.39	$170.39

Stop Loss AUD

	Signal	Actual Stop
Highest Close or HHV	$9.960	
Current ATR	$0.5300	
Quantity	270	
Initial Stop		$4.640
Breakeven Stop		$5.718
Chandelier Stop	3.0	$8.370
Current Stop Loss		$8.370

Sale 3

	AUD	AUD
Date		-
Exchange Rate	$1.0000	
Sale Price		$0.000
Brokerage	$0.00	
Other Fees	$0.00	
Quantity		0
Total Sale	$0.00	$0.00
Profit / Loss	$0.00	$0.00
% Return (on total trade value)		0.00%

Dividends Received

Ex Div Date	Ex Rate	Total Div	Franking %
2-May-04	$1.0000	$300.00	0%
	$1.0000		0%
	$1.0000		0%
	$1.0000		0%
	$1.0000		0%
Total Dividends		$300.00	$300.00

Margin Information

	AUD	AUD
LVR	90%	90%
Total Trade Value	$8,561.15	$8,561.15
Margin Amount	$7,619.13	$7,619.13
Capital Outlay	$942.02	$942.02

Rationale

Reason for entry:

Reason for exit:

Additional notes:

Business management

As part of managing your trading business there are specific activities that you need to undertake. They include:

- Regularly reviewing your current available capital and the risk levels of your open positions to determine if any new trades can be opened if an opportunity presents itself. I can simply look at the Totals worksheet on my *Smart Trader Spreadsheet* to check if I am fully invested or if I still have capital available. I also check where my current open market risk level is sitting (also called portfolio heat—this is covered in chapter 14). Figure 20.8 shows an example of the Totals worksheet from the *Smart Trader Spreadsheet*.

Figure 20.8: totals worksheet from the *Smart Trader Spreadsheet*

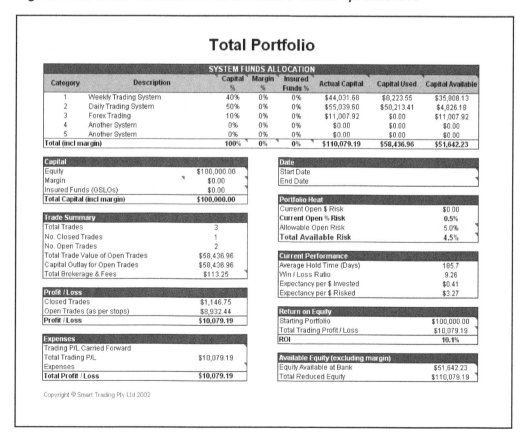

Total Portfolio

		SYSTEM FUNDS ALLOCATION					
Category	Description	Capital %	Margin %	Insured Funds %	Actual Capital	Capital Used	Capital Available
1	Weekly Trading System	40%	0%	0%	$44,031.68	$8,223.55	$35,808.13
2	Daily Trading System	50%	0%	0%	$55,039.60	$50,213.41	$4,826.18
3	Forex Trading	10%	0%	0%	$11,007.92	$0.00	$11,007.92
4	Another System	0%	0%	0%	$0.00	$0.00	$0.00
5	Another System	0%	0%	0%	$0.00	$0.00	$0.00
Total (incl margin)		100%	0%	0%	$110,079.19	$58,436.96	$51,642.23

Capital	
Equity	$100,000.00
Margin	$0.00
Insured Funds (GSLOs)	$0.00
Total Capital (incl margin)	**$100,000.00**

Trade Summary	
Total Trades	3
No. Closed Trades	1
No. Open Trades	2
Total Trade Value of Open Trades	$58,436.96
Capital Outlay for Open Trades	$58,436.96
Total Brokerage & Fees	$113.25

Profit / Loss	
Closed Trades	$1,146.75
Open Trades (as per stops)	$8,932.44
Profit / Loss	**$10,079.19**

Expenses	
Trading P/L Carried Forward	
Total Trading P/L	$10,079.19
Expenses	
Total Profit / Loss	**$10,079.19**

Date	
Start Date	
End Date	

Portfolio Heat	
Current Open $ Risk	$0.00
Current Open % Risk	**0.5%**
Allowable Open Risk	5.0%
Total Available Risk	**4.5%**

Current Performance	
Average Hold Time (Days)	185.7
Win / Loss Ratio	9.26
Expectancy per $ Invested	$0.41
Expectancy per $ Risked	$3.27

Return on Equity	
Starting Portfolio	$100,000.00
Total Trading Profit / Loss	$10,079.19
ROI	**10.1%**

Available Equity (excluding margin)	
Equity Available at Bank	$51,642.23
Total Reduced Equity	$110,079.19

- Balancing your accounts regularly. Active traders may do this once a month, whereas long-term traders may only do this once a year when they are getting their records together for their tax returns.

- Backing up your computer to protect your trading records (this is covered in chapter 22).

- Evaluating your performance as a trader and comparing your return with the benchmark that you set in your goals and objectives in chapter 4. I evaluate my performance by reviewing my statistics in the evaluation worksheet of the *Smart Trader Spreadsheet* (as shown in figure 21.2 on page 186). Measurements for trading performance are covered in chapter 21.

- Regularly reviewing your trading plan to remind yourself of your goals and updating it with any changes to your trading strategy. At first, your trading plan will be a work in progress—as you develop new skills and adapt your strategy, update your plan accordingly.

- Visiting your accountant at the end of each financial year to complete your annual tax return. You are required to lodge all your trading activities for the year with your return. This would be done in your personal name if you are a sole trader or as a separate entity if you are trading under a company, trust or self managed superannuation fund.

Improving your trading skills

In order to improve your performance in the market you need to continually develop your trading skills. As part of your trading routine you might make a goal of reading a book on trading or personal development once a month or once a quarter and undertaking a new course each year to assist you in developing and improving your trading skills and knowledge. You might also like to learn about different trading styles and different instruments and how other traders trade the markets to give you ideas and to find one that suits your personality. I teach my trading systems through a course called *Smart Trading Plan & System Development*—visit <www.smarttrading. com.au> for more information.

Developing your routine

Developing a trading routine is something that will evolve over time as you grow as a trader. What one trader does on a daily basis, another trader may do weekly or quarterly depending on his or her trading style and the instruments being traded. It is essential that you document your trading routine in your trading plan. Figure 20.9 is an example of a long-term investor's trading routine. Use this to guide you in documenting your own routine in your trading plan.

The length of time you spend on different trading activities each day, week, or month will depend on how often you trade. For short-term traders, particularly day traders, a daily trading routine may comprise a full day of work, from 9 am to 5 pm. The daily routine of a medium-term trader may take one to two hours, while a long-term trader may have no daily routine, working on a weekly basis instead.

Figure 20.9: sample routine from a trading plan for long-term investor

Trading routine

Daily routine

- If my weekly routine confirms I can open a new trade, I will review my watchlist folder and open a trade if a trigger presents itself.

Weekly routine

- Review the charts of my current open trades and determine whether any action should be taken, such as moving stop losses or adding more shares to a profitable trade.

- Update my Smart Trader Spreadsheet with any changes to my portfolio and check my current available capital and portfolio heat to see if I can open any new positions.

- Scan the market for long-term trading opportunities and add any shares that match my trading rules to my watchlist.

Monthly routine

- Review the charts of the world market indices and All Ords to determine the overall health and trend of the world markets.

- Review the charts of the major Australian sector indices to determine the overall health and trend of these sectors.

- Back up my computer.

Quarterly routine

- Read one book on the markets or enroll in a trading course to expand my trading knowledge and improve my skills.

Annual routine

- Review my yearly trading performance and total return on investment compared to the All Ords financial year performance. Did I meet my trading goals for the year? Do I need to make any changes to my trading strategy?

- Review my trading plan to remind myself of my goals and update it with any changes I have made to my trading strategy.

- With the assistance of an accountant, complete and submit my annual tax return.

✔ *Smart action step*

Start developing your trading routine. Keep in mind the style of trader that you have decided to be, your lifestyle and the amount of time that you have available to dedicate to trading. Ask yourself what you plan to do on a daily, weekly, monthly and quarterly basis and note these activities down in your *Smart Trading Plan Template*.

Part VII

Trading plan: analysis and backup

21

Trading performance and analysis

Trading is a business in itself and one of the keys to running a successful business is maintaining good records and regularly analysing your performance. You need to measure your actual trading performance—not just your bank account balance. This will show you the reality of how you are performing in the market and alert you to any changes that need to be made to your strategy.

Trades can be analysed when they are closed out as well as after a set period of trading—this may be monthly for a short-term trader, quarterly for a medium-term trader or yearly for a long-term trader.

After the trade

After you exit a trade you need to analyse and learn from it to identify any weaknesses or bad habits you are developing. Your trading experience is the best source of education and by analysing each trade, as well as tracking your entire trading results, you will get a feel for how you are performing in the market.

Ask yourself the following questions after each individual trade and note the answers in your trading diary:

- Did I identify a good trade?
- How good was my entry into the trade?
- Was my initial stop loss too wide or too tight?

- Did I move my stop to breakeven in a reasonable timeframe, or was it too early or too late?

- Was my trailing profit stop too wide or too tight?

- How good was my exit from the trade?

- What could I have done differently?

- How did I feel during the different stages of the trade?

- Did I follow my trading plan?

In my early days of trading I had a self-awareness journal that I would write in at the end of each trading day, answering the above questions whenever I closed out a trade. This is how I came to recognise my weaknesses and understand my patterns, as outlined in chapter 2.

Your goal with this analysis is to identify and understand where any weaknesses may lie in your trading so that you can learn to overcome these and turn them into strengths. It is easy to develop bad trading habits—by studying each trade you may identify patterns such as closing out trades before your stop is hit and not letting your profits run. Another bad habit is not exiting when the trade hits your stop loss and hanging on in hope. Maybe you are getting anxious or becoming afraid of the market? It is important to track your emotions prior to, during and after the trade and study your reactions. Ask yourself why you keep doing these things and aim to develop better trading habits so that you can become a peak performer in the markets. You need to train yourself as a trader, just as an athlete trains to become a top performer in his or her chosen sport.

Total performance evaluation

To analyse your trading performance and decide what, if any, improvements need to be made, you will need to review at least 20 trades for the figure to be statistically significant. It may take anywhere from a few months to a year to build up this amount of trades.

In his book *Trading in the Zone*, Mark Douglas explains why 20 trades is an adequate sample size. If you haven't read his book you must do so—it is one of the top books on the psychology of trading. The author actually recommends that (after you've got your trading plan together) you undertake 20 trades, exactly as per your plan, and do not deviate from this number. Then review your results after those 20 trades and determine if you've got an edge in the market that puts the odds in your favour. Mark describes trading as a game of probabilities, not much different to playing a poker machine.

Performance measures include:

- profitability—return on investment
- reliability—the number of winning trades compared with the number of losing trades
- average win size
- average loss size
- win to loss size
- average hold time
- equity curve.

As part of your trading routine, make a habit of calculating these measurements on a regular basis and compare the results with your previous performance. Your performance will vary as market conditions continually change. Trends will emerge over time and will assist you in identifying any weaknesses in your trading strategy and determining if you need to take appropriate action.

Let's have a look at the different types of measurements in more detail. I have included some sample trading results to give you a better idea of how these measurements are calculated.

Profitability: return on investment

It is important that you are always aware of how profitable your business of trading is. This can be tracked as both a dollar and a percentage figure and is simply the amount you have gained or lost over a set period. For example, let's say you have a trading capital of $100 000 and you have made over $16 000 in a year:

Trading capital:	$100 000
Net trading profits:	$16 229
Net percentage return:	16.2 per cent (profits ÷ trading capital) x 100

If you set yourself a benchmark in your trading returns and objectives (as outlined in chapter 4), did you achieve this goal? If you did, give yourself a pat on the back and reward yourself for your trading efforts. You need to celebrate your success and make a habit of doing so as you achieve your goals.

If you did not achieve your goal, was your benchmark too high? Do you have unrealistic expectations of what trading could bring you? Did you follow your trading plan? Do you think you can achieve the benchmark in the future? If you believe you can, find ways to improve your trading performance so that you can achieve your benchmark.

The next step is to delve into your profitability further and understand how your profits were made or (if it was a negative return) how your losses were made and where you went wrong. In order to be successful in the markets you need to have a positive return and if you don't achieve this you will have to either cease trading or find ways to top up your trading account. But just topping up your account does not ensure future success—take a serious look at your trading and work out why you have achieved a negative return. The following statistics will help you to understand and pinpoint where your weaknesses lie.

Reliability: win to loss probabilities

Your reliability is basically the number of winning trades divided by your total number of trades, compared with your number of losing trades divided by your total number of trades. Let's assume that you have undertaken 20 trades and these were your results:

Total number of trades undertaken: 20

Number of winning trades: 12

Number of losing trades: 8

To calculate your reliability, divide your winning trades by the total number of trades then multiply this by 100. Do the same for your losing trades:

Probability of winning trades: (12 ÷ 20) x 100 = 60 per cent

Probability of losing trades: (8 ÷ 20) x 100 = 40 per cent

Based on this information your probability of undertaking a winning trade is 60 per cent—that's a good reliability.

Don't be alarmed if your result is under 50 per cent. It is a fact that most professional traders run at a reliability of 50 per cent or less, but their secret is ensuring that their average win size is much larger than their average loss size. This ensures that they are profitable in the long term.

Win to loss size

Your percentage of winning trades is one thing, but your win to loss size is more important. This will determine if you have been successful in the markets and will continue to be successful. To calculate this measurement you firstly need to calculate your average win size and your average loss size.

Average win size

To work out your average win size, add up all your profits from your winning trades (after brokerage costs) and divide these by the number of winning trades to get your average size.

Total profits on winning trades:	$22090
Total winning trades:	12
Average winning trade:	$22090 ÷ 12 = $1840.83

Average loss size

Do the same for your losing trades—add up all the losses that you undertook with your losing trades (after brokerage) and divide this by your number of losing trades.

Total losses on losing trades:	$5861
Total losing trades:	8
Average losing trade:	$5861 ÷ 8 = $732.63

Win to loss size ratio

Now you can divide your average win size by your average loss size to get the win to loss size ratio.

Average win size:	$1840.83
Average loss size:	$732.63
Win to loss size ratio:	$1840.83 ÷ $732.63 = 2.51

A win to loss size ratio of 2.51 is excellent, because it means that your winners are much larger than your losses. Even if you have a reliability under 50 per cent, you would still be profitable in the long term because your average win size is more than double your average loss size.

To put it into perspective, if you have a reliability of 50 per cent and a win to loss size ratio of one, this would mean your win size was exactly the same as your loss size and you would simply be breaking even. The more you can increase your win size, the larger your profits will be.

On the other hand, if your win to loss size is below one, this means your losing trades are larger than your winning trades and you need to take immediate action to understand why this has occurred, otherwise you will not survive in the market. Is your position sizing too large? Are you cutting your winning trades short and taking profits too early? Or maybe you are not acting on stops. Psychologically you may be lacking discipline.

Your goal should be to keep your win size much larger than your loss size. The only way you can do this is to let your profits run in the market and keep your losses small. You don't want those losses to get out of hand.

Successful trading is all about following that golden rule of trading and position sizing all trades based on a small percentage of risk with a clear stop-loss management strategy.

Average hold time

The next measurement to consider is your average hold time in the market. This is another way to see if things are going wrong. Determine how active a trader you are by looking at your timeframes and average hold time for both your winning and losing trades.

To calculate your average hold time, add together all the days (including weekends) that you held each trade open for and divide this by the total number of trades. This tells you the average length of time you keep a trade open for, irrelevant of whether it is a winning trade or a losing trade. For example:

Total days each trade was open:	320 days
Total number of trades:	20
Average hold time per trade:	320 ÷ 20 = 16 days

This will give you an idea of what timeframe trader you actually are. You might be surprised to see that, although you thought you were a long-term trader, your average hold time shows that you are not.

Break this figure down further by looking at your average hold time for your winning trades and losing trades.

Average hold time per winning trade

Add up the total days all your winning trades were open and divide this by your number of winning trades.

Total days winning trades were open:	240 days
Total number of winning trades:	12
Average hold time per winning trade:	240 ÷ 12 = 20 days

Average hold time per losing trade

Add up the total days all your losing trades were open and divide this by your number of losing trades.

Total days losing trades were open:	80 days
Total number of losing trades:	8
Average hold time per losing trade:	80 ÷ 8 = 10 days

By understanding your average hold time you can really get a feel for the timeframe that you're trading and get an idea of how long you hold winning trades versus losing trades. You can then bring this information into play with your statistics. In the above example, the average hold time for winning trades was double that of losing trades, which shows that the losing trades are being cut short and the winning trades held longer to let the profits run.

If you have a low win to loss size, you must find out why this is occurring. If you find that your average hold time on your losing trades is larger than your winning trades, ask yourself why this is so. Are you hanging on in the hope that things will improve and you won't have to take a loss? Or are you taking profits too early on your winning trades and not letting those profits run? By delving into your average hold times you can see if there are any patterns.

Equity curve

An equity curve is a visual representation of your trading performance that you chart on a regular basis as your equity changes. Initially, you plot your open equity (initial trading capital) and then once a month (or once a quarter) you plot the value of your current equity at that point in time and see how this changes over time. Your current trading equity will be based on any money still in your bank account plus the value of your open portfolio. Your equity curve will either be rising or falling, depending on your trading performance. Your goal is to have a nice and steady rising equity curve. This can be hard to achieve, especially when you are still learning and experiencing periods of choppiness. This will be reflected in the shape of your equity curve.

The *Smart Trader Spreadsheet* makes this very easy to do. You simply enter your trading capital balance at the end of each month and it plots it for you on a chart that displays the changes in your equity, as shown in figure 21.1.

Figure 21.1: example of the ECurve worksheet from the *Smart Trader Spreadsheet*

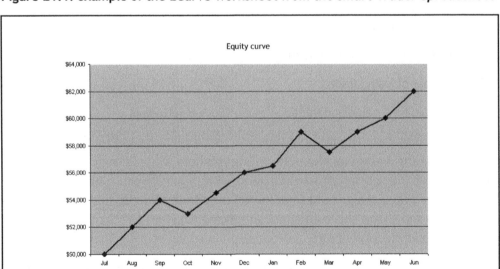

Cost of trading

Unfortunately, trading is not a zero-sum game. Every time you open a trade in the market you are automatically a net loser—if the trade doesn't immediately rise from the moment you open it, you will have lost money due to the brokerage costs. Every time you take a losing trade you have to make up for the loss as well as the brokerage costs on the next trade. This can have a negative impact on your profitability as a trader, especially if you have a small account size and are paying large brokerage costs.

Brokerage costs are just part of the business of trading and should be taken into account with your statistics. The *Smart Trader Spreadsheet* does this for me. I simply enter the brokerage costs when I open and close a trade on the Trade worksheet (as shown in figure 20.7 on page 170) and it factors this cost into my trading results and provides a total of these costs on the Totals worksheet (as shown in figure 20.8 on page 171). Just be aware that the more you trade, the more brokerage you are going to pay and this will have an impact on your results. If you are a short-term trader who is very active in the market, you will be surprised how the costs of trading add up and this can affect your overall performance results.

Keep good records

All of this analysis will take time and effort to perform. Trading is not an easy endeavour and to succeed you have to be prepared to put in the effort and track your trades through a good record-keeping structure.

As mentioned previously, the easiest way to track your trades and manage your risk on an ongoing basis is to keep a trading diary of some form that you use to record all your trades, manage your risk and track your performance. This could be an exercise book or an Excel spreadsheet. As you are aware, I use the *Smart Trader Spreadsheet* (visit <www.smarttrading.com.au> for more information on this product).

Your trading diary should cover the following information for each trade you undertake. This will enable you to pre-plan and track each trade.

- Why did you enter the trade?

- Where is your initial stop loss set?

- What percentage of capital are you risking on this trade?

- How many shares did you purchase based on this?

- At what point will you move your stop to breakeven?

- At what point will you move your stop to a trailing profit stop?

- Will you pyramid and add to this position?

- If so, when will you pyramid?

- What will you risk on the pyramid position and how many shares will you buy?

- Why did you exit the trade?

Also keep track of your total capital invested and portfolio heat, so you can manage your maximum risk across your portfolio and ensure you don't trade beyond your means. The *Smart Trader Spreadsheet* manages all of this for me. I simply view the Totals worksheet to see this information (as shown in figure 20.7 on page 170).

Once you've built up a good sample group of trades you can analyse your performance as a trader and recognise if things are going well or if you need to take immediate action to address any problems. That is why it is important to keep good records. Your results will not lie and will tell you if you are currently a peak performer or not. To analyse my performance I simply view the Evaluation worksheet (as shown in figure 21.2) in the *Smart Trader Spreadsheet* once a quarter. It is set up to calculate all the measurements that have been covered in this chapter, plus much more.

Figure 21.2: evaluation worksheet from the *Smart Trader Spreadsheet*

Evaluation of Total Trading Activity

Profitability	
Trading profits / losses	$10,377.16
Trading capital	$100,000.00
Actual capital outlaid for period	$3,384.49
Total trade value for period	$72,846.36
% Return on trading capital	10.38%
% Return on capital outlay	306.61%

Trade Period	
Start date	0-Jan-00
End date	0-Jan-00

Total Trades	
Total number of trades	3
Average trade hold time (days)	191.7

Winning Trades	
Total number of winning trades	2
Probability of winning trades	66.67%
Average win size	$5,615.21
Average win per $ invested	$5.92
Average win per $ risked	$5.33
Average winning trade hold time	238.5

Losing Trades	
Total number of losing trades	1
Probability of losing trades	33.33%
Average loss size	$853.25
Average loss per $ invested	$0.59
Average loss per $ risked	$0.84
Average losing trade hold time	98.0

Average Wins : Losses	
Average profit / loss per trade	$4,761.96
Average win to average loss ratio	6.58

Mood Ranking	
How I felt during the trading period:	
(scale 1 to 10, 1 worst & 10 best)	

Figure 21.3 shows an example of how you would document your trade evaluation in your trading plan. Set yourself a goal to do this on a regular basis.

Figure 21.3: sample statement from a trading plan for a long-term investor

Trade evaluation

I will make a regular habit of reviewing each trade as I close it out to determine if I am developing any bad habits in the market.

I will use the Smart Trader Spreadsheet to track and manage all my trading activity in the market and assess my profitability and review my trading performance on a yearly basis.

If my statistics and trade analysis show that things are going wrong I will take a step back from my trading and reassess myself and my trading systems.

✔ *Smart action step*

As part of your trading routine, develop a record-keeping structure to track all your trades and analyse your trading performance on a regular basis.

22

Contingency plans

One of the keys to success is knowing how to respond to the unexpected. You need to consider everything that could possibly go wrong in your business of trading and determine how you will respond to each situation by having a contingency plan to protect you.

What if your computer crashes or is stolen? What if your broker's website goes down and you can't place a trade? What if your internet connection or means of communication to your broker is cut off? What if a severe price shock or market crash occurs? How will you respond in these situations?

If you have read Van Tharp's book *Trade Your Way to Financial Freedom*, you would understand how important this is. He writes that traders should be emotionally and mentally prepared for the absolute worst-case scenarios and unexpected events that could occur. He says to '*plan your responses in your mind and rehearse them*'—just like undertaking a fire drill.

Back up everything

Owners of successful businesses undertake regular backups to protect their data. If you use your computer to trade the markets, run market scans, manage your trading portfolio and write your trading plan, then you want to protect this information. You have probably heard of people who have lost everything on their computer due to a virus or a thunderstorm—or perhaps it has happened to you.

If it does happen, how will you retrieve this information? How are you going to handle things in the meantime until your computer is back up and running? How will you manage your stop losses and your portfolio during that time? Do you have a laptop available? If anything like this does happen, it is probably best to take a step back from the market and just manage your open trades until you have it all sorted out.

There are plenty of ways to back up computers these days. You can copy everything onto a DVD, a memory stick or a separate hard drive. Use your common sense — don't leave your backups in your laptop bag with your laptop or next to your computer. It is best to store them in a separate location because you might lose them too if there is a fire or your computer is stolen. It is not until something happens that you realise the importance of regularly backing up your computer files.

Internet connections

Another thing to consider as part of your contingency plan is what to do if your broker's website goes offline and you can't access the trading platform. This has happened to me a few times. It's important to make sure you can trade over the phone — keep the relevant phone numbers handy so you can easily call your broker and place a trade or take action on an existing trade.

What will you do if your internet connection goes down? If you use broadband, can you arrange a dial-up internet account to use in emergencies? Ask your internet provider if they offer this in these situations. If not, can you set up an account that you only pay for if you use it?

Power outages

What if there is a power outage and your electricity supply shuts down? No problem, you might say — you just won't trade. However, what if you were in a situation where you had just entered a trade? This happened to me.

I was intraday trading with CFDs when they were free to deal with many years back. Intraday trading means you close out the trade by the end of the day and don't hold any positions overnight. I had just entered a trade when my computer shut down — I realised there was a blackout in the house. I had not yet set the stop loss, which is a critical part of my trading and absolutely necessary for an intraday trade. Thinking 'What am I going to do now?', I picked up the phone to call my broker, only to discover that it didn't work either. It was a remote phone that required electricity to operate, not a landline that worked without power. I then picked up my mobile phone, and guess what—the battery was flat and it didn't work. I ended up running to the garage and plugging my mobile phone into the car to give the battery some power so I could call my broker and exit the trade.

It's not until something like this happens that you realise how important it is to have a contingency plan. Since this situation occurred, I now have a landline phone that requires no power to operate and a UPS power plug. This is an uninterrupted power supply that gives me half an hour battery backup when the power goes out and is also a surge protector to protect my computer during storms and power surges. You can buy this unit at most electrical retailers.

Handling a market crash

What if there is a huge drop in the Dow Jones overnight and it falls 5 per cent or more in value—how are you going to react in this situation? This would cause alarm when the Australian market opens because people would panic and start selling—it's the herd mentality. This has occurred a few times in the last 25 years, most notably after the World Trade Center attacks. This, however, was a unique event and there are usually no signs in the market when a terrorist attack occurs. Market crashes, on the other hand, usually display signs of a pending change in trend. For technical traders, the signs can be found in the charts of the major indices. They start to form top patterns such as double tops and a break of support or break of a major uptrend line is usually an unhealthy sign for the markets.

Personally, I know that if my stop losses are hit I will automatically exit. Stop losses are my lifeline in the market no matter what happens. My weekly routine of keeping an eye on the world indices and local market indices alerts me to the signs of a market change. If I see a shift in market strength to the short side and I receive signals to short sell shares (short selling was covered chapter 16), I will commence opening positions on that side of the market. I am usually stopped out of any long trades I have open—this occurred in the market drop in January 2008. I had predominantly short trades open and was able to profit from the large fall that occurred. It was my trading routine, market scans and risk management that ensured I was facing in the right direction during this time to profit from the large drop.

Events like this demonstrate how important it is to manage your ongoing risk in the market and not overexpose yourself. You never know what is just around the corner in the markets. Figure 22.1 shows an example statement from a trading plan to guide you in completing this information in your own trading plan.

Figure 22.1: sample statement from a trading plan for a long-term investor

Contingency plan

As part of my monthly routine I will regularly make backups of my computer files and store them in a separate location.

I have equipment in place to protect me if there is a power surge or power outage and a dial-up internet connection as backup in case broadband connection problems occur. I will keep my broker's phone number handy so that I can call to make any changes to my portfolio during these times.

I know that no matter what happens, my stop losses rule and will tell me when to exit. By managing my maximum open market risk through portfolio heat I will never be overexposed in the marketplace and will be aware of my worst-case scenario at all times.

✔ *Smart action step*

Consider all the worst-case scenarios that could occur in your trading business and how you will react to them. Play them out in your mind and set up an action plan that details what you will do if they ever occur.

23

Personal rules

The last page of your trading plan can be a list of your personal rules. This is where you can include personal reminders to yourself that don't fit into other areas of your plan. If you notice any weaknesses or any bad habits in your trading, you may want to put some rules in this section to help you overcome those weaknesses and remind yourself not to do certain things. If you find an inspiring quote in a book, include it in this part of your plan. It's a section that you can complete as you desire.

I want to share with you the personal rules that I had in my original trading plan. They reflect my evolution as a trader. I continued to add to them as I recognised weaknesses, and they evolved from entries, to exits to psychology and mindset. They also reinforce what trading is all about and summarise many of the concepts I have already covered in this book.

Never override your trading system

I spent a lot of time developing my systems and back-testing them over a range of markets so I could understand how they performed and gain confidence in them. It was then a matter of ensuring I had the discipline to follow these rules and never override them.

Remember that patience is the key to success

I had very little patience when I first started trading. I wanted it all to happen instantly and the more impatient I was, the less success I had. I became sidetracked and turned to short-term trading and options. I thought I was going to make money fast, when in actual fact it didn't work like that at all—it was emotional trading. Once I came to see this, I switched to just trading my systems and following my rules without deviation. Only then did the money begin to flow.

Accept small losses cheerfully as a fact of life

Unfortunately, losses are part of the trading game and you're going to experience them—there is nothing you can do about it. I now consider losses as the market's way of telling me that the trade was no good and it is giving me my money back to put into something better and bring me closer to the next big winner.

Always be a trend follower—never trade against the trend

As the saying goes, 'the trend is your friend'. I aim to take the highest reward trades by trading in the direction of the trend and, for my long-term system, sticking with it until it ends.

Do not overtrade

As you know, trading is not a zero-sum game. Every trade you open in the market costs you money. There are brokerage costs attached to both entering and exiting a trade. Losses do add up and so do the brokerage costs.

Don't worry about missing a trade—the market will always be there

If there are no attractive trading opportunities available, you don't have to trade. The market will be open five days a week for your entire life, so you don't have to trade every day. Just trade the strong moves when they occur.

Don't exit just to take profits—there could be more profits to be had

Exiting early was one of my biggest weaknesses. There is nothing worse than watching a share continue to go your way after you have exited. As long as the share is continuing to trend, don't rush to take profits. Only exit when an exit signal is given. It took me a long time to learn this, but once I started sticking to the rule of just following the trend and following my trailing stop, the money began to flow in. There will only be a few big winners that make you the big money and if you cut them short, you're not going to be able to make great returns in the market.

Remember that money cannot be made every day in the markets

Big moves take time to develop and a share may not immediately go your way after you purchase it. As long as it does start to go your way at some stage and enables you to raise your stop loss, then that's a good sign.

Be aware that the probability of a 'win' is insignificant

The size of your wins is more important than your number of wins to losses. It is the large win sizes that will make you the big money in the market.

Do not judge your next trade on the basis of your last trade

Just because something happened with one trade doesn't mean it's going to happen with another trade. Smash those rear-view mirrors.

Remember that price is irrelevant

It doesn't matter whether you think a share is expensive or cheap. If the share continues to rise, the price is irrelevant. You may have thought Rio Tinto was too expensive to buy at $50, $70 and $80, but I bet you were kicking yourself when the price rose over $100 and higher still. On the other hand, if a share is falling, you don't know how low it's going to go. Don't buy a share just because you think it's cheap. It could become cheaper still, or even become insolvent and delist from the stock market, just like One.Tel and HIH Insurance.

Act like a master trader

Before you take any action in the market, ask yourself, 'Am I acting like a master trader by doing this? Would a professional trader do the same?' Put your professional trading hat on and tell yourself, 'I'm a professional trader and I want to trade like one'. Gain control over your emotions and act professionally in the markets. If you do things that a professional trader wouldn't do, you are not going to succeed in the market and are simply sabotaging yourself.

Never hesitate—when you see a signal, act on it

One of my goals was to become automatic in my trading. If I get a signal and I like it, I want to act on it immediately and take the trade. When my stop loss is hit, I want to exit without hesitation.

Never fear success

Visualise your life in a positive way and imagine how you want it to be. If you don't think you are worthy enough to be making money in trading, you are not going to do well. You won't be attracted to the top winning trades. It's all about the law of attraction. See yourself as a successful trader now and know that you can make the returns and outperform your set benchmark.

Recognise when to stay out of the market

If the market conditions are unfavourable or you are emotionally distracted or ill and can't focus on the market, just take a step back. Don't worry about missing opportunities; the market will still be there when you are emotionally ready to start trading again. Know when to trade and when not to trade.

Plan each trade and trade each plan

All trades should be planned in advance — the reason for entry, how much to commit to the trade, the stop-loss strategy and a fallback if things go wrong. Once you have determined a strategy, make sure you have the discipline to stick to it.

Always analyse winners and losers, but never agonise over them

Wins and losses are equally a part of trading. Make sure you win bigger than you lose, let your profits run, learn from your mistakes and reward your successes.

Remember that you are the most important factor in your trading performance

Your trading results are ultimately your responsibility and you need to find ways to improve your behaviour in the markets. Success or failure in the markets depends on your overall mindset. Take the time to complete a trading plan and have the discipline and self-control to follow that plan.

✔ *Smart action step*

Start adding personal rules to your *Smart Trading Plan Template*. As you recognise weaknesses or bad habits developing in your trading, add a rule to this section of your plan to remind yourself not to do it again.

Part VIII Review

24

Real trading

> **Justine achieves top 5 per cent ranking in**
>
> **CMC Markets Trading Competition with an 82 per cent return**

In 2007, CMC Markets (a CFD provider) ran a trading competition over an eight-week period. I decided to participate in the competition, trading under the nickname of 'Justdoit'. I undertook 20 share CFD trades using my daily trading system and achieved a fantastic return of 82.47 per cent, which put me in 22nd place out of 438 competitors.

Figure 24.1 (overleaf) is an image from the CMC Markets competition website that shows my ranking and results at the end of the competition. After the competition ended in late May, I continued holding my open positions and increased this return to 155 per cent.

Figure 24.1: CMC Markets competition result

ATTENTION COMPETITORS: THIS IS YOUR R.O.I

Nickname	ROI	Position
justdoit	82.47%	22%

© CMC Markets. Reproduced with permission

My results and trading history from this competition provide a great opportunity to show you how returns like this can be achieved by following your trading system and managing your risks. I would like to share with you a summary of my trades and look at some of the major trades in more detail. Firstly, let me give you a brief overview of my trading systems so that you have a better idea of how I trade the markets.

My trading systems

I trade the markets with two systems and have a mechanical approach. My approach is very simple and is based around trading trends and using strict money management rules to follow that golden rule of trading: letting your profits run and cutting your losses short.

I use MetaStock with a mechanical filter to scan for entries (I covered how to run a scan using MetaStock in chapter 20) and a trailing stop loss indicator for exits. I also incorporate a range of money management techniques to size my trades, manage my open market risk and maximise my winning positions through pyramiding, strategies that are all covered in this book.

Figures 24.2 and 24.3 (on pages 201 and 202) are visual representations of the two systems I have developed and personally use. The entry signals provided by the system are denoted by an arrow and the exit is shown by the line under the share price. Each time you see a small arrow on the charts, this means the share gave me a buy signal and would have shown up in my report from the MetaStock scan when I ran it that day or week (for my weekly system). My goal is to enter on one of the first few entry signals provided and exit when it crosses the trailing stop-loss line. This is a simple approach that makes trading easy.

The first system I trade is my weekly long-term trend-following system, as shown in figure 24.2. The weekly system keeps me in the long-term trend of the share and enables me to remain with the trade until it becomes unhealthy and an exit signal is provided. The hold time ranges from a few months to a year or two. This system involves running a MetaStock scan on the weekends to search for shares that meet certain entry criteria. It requires approximately one hour's work per week.

Figure 24.2: weekly trading system sample chart

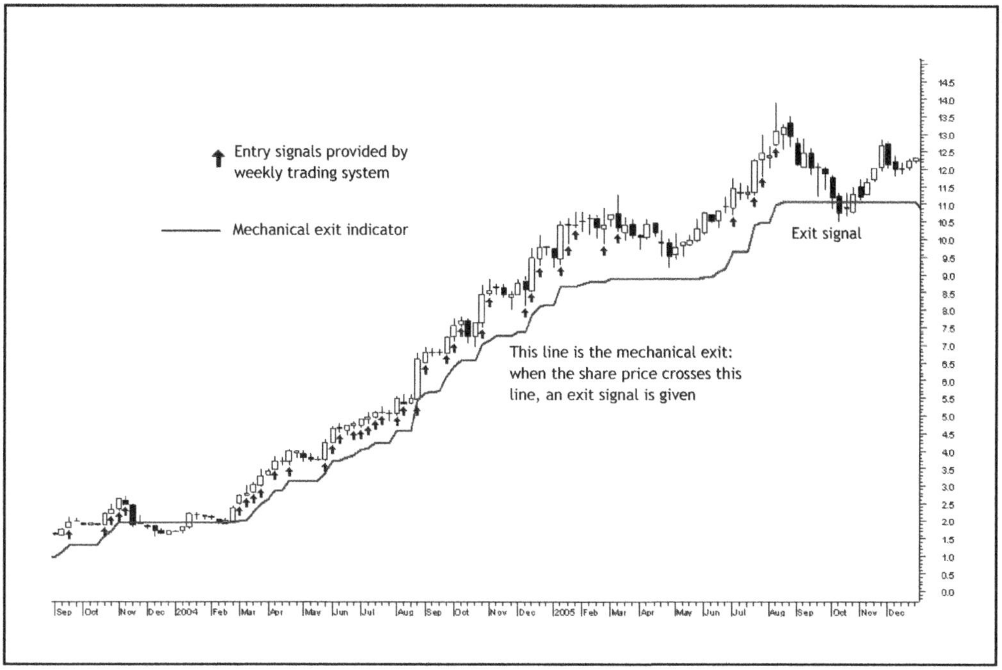

The second system is my daily breakout system, as shown in figure 24.3 (overleaf). The goal of this system is to trade a swing move in an already-trending share. It is ideal for trading CFDs and has an average hold time of four to six weeks. The system involves running a scan once a day and takes less than one hour's work per day. This is the system that I used during the CMC Markets competition in 2007.

Figure 24.3: daily trading system sample chart

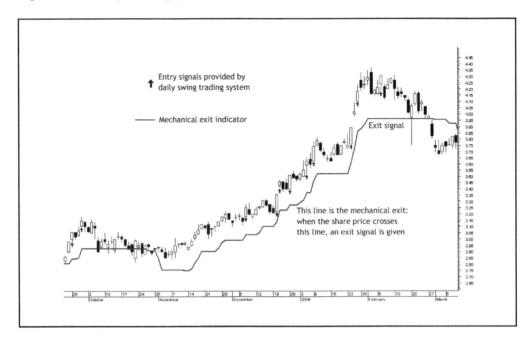

I trade both systems long and short. I cover all the details of my trading strategies and systems in the *Smart Trading Plan & System Development Course* that I have developed (you can find out more by visiting <www.smarttrading.com.au>).

CMC Markets Trading Competition

The CMC Markets competition ran for eight weeks from 2 April to 31 May 2007. A total of 438 competitors participated in the competition and it involved real CFD trading with your own personal CMC Markets trading account.

For more information on the competition, including extensive interviews with the winner and runners-up, pick up a copy of *Real Traders II* by Eva Diaz.

The only prerequisite for participation was that you had a CMC trading account with a minimum of $5000 in total equity. There was a prize of $100000 for the trader with the highest return on investment at the end of the competition.

Remember, CFDs are highly margined. With CMC Markets you can trade with as little as 3 per cent down on a trade. So a $5000 trading account would enable you to open trades to the value of over $100 000.

I allocated myself a total trading account of $100 000 for the competition and I put 10 per cent of this in my CMC Markets account. The remaining $90 000 was invested into a high-yield interest-earning account to offset the interest costs I was paying on a daily basis for my CFD trades. The interest rate was 8.25 per cent per annum and this was debited from my trading account balance on a daily basis.

I undertook a total of 20 trades during the competition. They were all long trades because the overall market strength during the competition was bullish and this is where my system was providing the strongest signals.

My strategy was to use my daily trading system and position size all my trades, risking 1.5 per cent of my total trading account ($1500) and ensuring no single position exceeded 20 per cent of my total capital ($20 000). I managed every trade based on my trailing stop and time stop, which I set to three weeks during the competition.

My statistics

By the end of the competition on 31 May I had increased my $10 000 account to over $18 000, which equated to an 82.47 per cent return. Table 24.1 (overleaf) shows a summary of my statistics when the competition ended and where they finished up when the last trade was closed. Because the competition involved real trading, I continued to let my profits run on nine trades after the competition ended and exited the last trade on 31 July 2007.

The returns on the trades that were still open at the end of the competition are based on the closing price of the share as of 31 May.

As you can see from these statistics, I was not an aggressive trader and did not do any day trading. I only traded share CFDs and I was very pleased to achieve the position I did in the competition without the need to trade aggressive instruments in a short timeframe.

During the competition I had an average hold time of 22 days, which is just over three weeks.

Table 24.1: my competition statistics

Details	End of competition 31/5/07	Last trade exited 31/7/07
Account balance at start of competition	$10 055.08	—
Final account balance	$18 347.18	$25 632.91
Profit	$8292.10	$15 577.83
Percentage return	82.47%	154.92%
Trade period	2 months	4 months
Total no. of trades	20	20
Total no. of winning trades	9 (45%)	9 (45%)
Total no. of losing trades	11 (55%)	11 (55%)
Largest win	$4923.00	$10 974.91
Largest loss	$1376.06	$1376.06
Average win size	$1899.15	$2544.20
Average loss size	$656.88	$605.07
Average win to loss size ratio	2.9	4.1
Average trade hold time	22 days	34 days
Average winning trade hold time	23 days	41 days
Average losing trade hold time	21 days	28 days

By the time all 20 trades were closed on 31 July, I had increased my account balance to over $25 000, which equates to a total return of 155 per cent on my opening balance. My return had nearly doubled two months after the competition ended from the nine trades that I continued to let run.

Personally, I always look at returns based on the total capital I am using to position size my trades. I allocated myself a total trading account of $100000 for the competition and was predominantly fully invested at all times. My return on this total capital amount equates to 15 per cent over the four-month period.

During this time (2 April to 31 July 2007) the All Ords rose a total of 3.5 per cent, which means I outperformed the major index. This is my benchmark for judging my trading returns.

Not every trade I undertook was a winner. Of the 20 trades I opened, nine were winning trades and 11 were losing trades, or 45 per cent were winners and 55 per cent were losers. Losses are an inevitable part of trading and if these are kept small and profits large, then you will be successful.

As I mentioned in chapter 21, most professional traders run at a reliability of 50 per cent or less, but their secret is ensuring that their average win size is much larger than their average loss size and this can only be achieved by letting profits run. This was evident in my average hold time and my average win to loss size ratio.

My average hold time on all trades was 34 days, with the winning trades being held for an average of 41 days and the losing trades for 28 days. As the statistics show, I held my winning trades for much longer than my losing trades and my final win to loss size ratio increased to 4.1.

By continuing to let my profits run on my nine remaining trades after the competition ended, I was able to increase my win to loss size ratio to above 4. This means my win size is more than four times my loss size. That's what provided me with the returns in this competition and continues to do so in my trading as a whole.

Trade summary

As I have mentioned previously, the reality of trading is that it will only be a few trades that make you the big money and you need to stick with them. I had three top winning trades in the competition that provided me with a large return and I broke even on all the rest—with a few small profits and losses scattered across the other trades. Table 24.2 (overleaf) shows a summary of all my trades and their results when I exited them (including the nine that I exited after the competition ended on 31 May). They are listed in order of return, from highest to lowest.

Table 24.2: summary of trades

Details		Opening position				Closing position				Review	
Code	Open date	Quantity	Entry price	Margin %	Capital outlay	Close date	Quantity	Exit price	Hold time	Profit / loss	ROI
QGC	15/05/07	9500	$1.79	10%	$1717.50	9/07/07	11500	$2.88	55	$10974.91	490.94%
	18/06/07	2000	$2.54	10%	$518.00						
FMG	7/05/07	500	$26.00	5%	$663.00	14/05/07	250	$32.34			
						21/05/07	250	$33.77	14	$3494.50	527.07%
IIN	7/05/07	7000	$1.59	10%	$1124.13	6/06/07	7000	$2.07	30	$3334.38	296.62%
SDG	11/05/07	4500	$3.49	5%	$800.96	31/07/07	4500	$3.89	81	$1766.79	220.58%
AOE	29/03/07	5500	$1.73	50%	$4767.50	27/04/07	5500	$1.90	29	$898.08	18.84%
NAB	10/04/07	650	$42.06	3%	$847.51	10/05/07	650	$43.46	30	$854.41	100.81%
AWE	22/05/07	5500	$3.25	5%	$911.62	27/07/07	5500	$3.38	66	$697.13	76.47%
UGL	4/05/07	1200	$16.08	5%	$984.09	5/06/07	1200	$16.68	32	$680.70	69.17%
BKN	11/04/07	1500	$9.28	5%	$709.92	16/05/07	1500	$9.43	35	$196.94	27.74%
ANZ	16/04/07	1000	$30.80	3%	$954.80	10/05/07	1000	$30.76	24	−$101.56	−10.64%
TCL	18/04/07	2000	$8.17	5%	$833.34	14/05/07	2000	$8.12	26	−$132.58	−15.91%
OXR	10/04/07	5000	$3.22	5%	$821.10	25/05/07	5000	$3.19	45	−$182.05	−22.17%
CPU	17/05/07	1500	$11.56	5%	$884.34	26/06/07	1500	$11.44	40	−$214.50	−24.26%
WAN	4/04/07	700	$16.85	5%	$601.37	14/05/07	700	$16.42	40	−$320.78	−53.34%
KZL	23/05/07	2000	$7.02	10%	$1418.04	26/06/07	2000	$6.78	34	−$507.60	−35.80%
BTA	2/05/07	6000	$1.80	10%	$1087.77	24/05/07	6000	$1.69	22	−$650.91	−59.84%
DJS	14/05/07	3000	$5.35	5%	$819.16	13/06/07	3000	$5.14	30	−$673.48	−82.22%
CGJ	2/05/07	1500	$17.73	5%	$1356.34	29/05/07	1500	$16.96	27	−$1207.03	−88.99%
AXA	23/05/07	2500	$8.09	5%	$1031.47	7/06/07	2500	$7.59	15	−$1289.19	−124.99%
TAH	4/05/07	1000	$18.70	5%	$953.70	16/05/07	1000	$17.36	12	−$1376.06	−144.29%

My largest win was with Queensland Gas Company (QGC) which generated a profit of $10974. My largest loss was with Tabcorp (TAH), which generated a loss of $1376 and was below my allocated risk value of $1500 per trade. As you can see my top winners were multiples of my risk value and my losses came in lower than my risk value. Below is more detailed information on my top three winning trades and my largest losing trade.

Trade 1: Fortescue Metals Group (FMG)

FMG was my big winner of the competition because I opened and closed the trade within the competition timeframe. On 7 May I ran a daily scan (which I do each day at 3.30 pm) across the CMC custom folder of share CFDs. I reviewed all the opportunities from the report generated by the scan and the two trades that appealed to me based on my visual trading plan rules that day were Fortescue Metals Group (FMG) and IINet (IIN).

FMG was in an established uptrend but it had paused and trended sideways for six weeks. It developed a short-term resistance level at $24.00. When it broke through this resistance and moved to new highs, my system gave me a buy signal and I bought 500 CFDs.

I position sized the trade using the percentage of equity model, risking 1.5 per cent of my total trading capital. I set an initial stop loss below resistance at $23.32. The margin on this CFD was 5 per cent, which is what I was required to outlay to open the trade. The details of my trade entry are summarised below.

Entry date:	7 May 2007
Buy price:	$26.00
Initial stop loss:	$23.32
Risk:	$2.68 ($26.00 − $23.32)
Risk value:	$1500.00
No. of shares:	560
Actual purchased:	500
Total trade size:	$13000.00
Margin:	5%
Brokerage costs:	$13.00
Capital outlay on trade:	$663.00

I managed the trade using my mechanical trailing stop loss. The share rose phenomenally fast and just went up day after day. It is hard not to get excited when you get into a trade like this one and you are in the nice position of raising your stop price on a daily basis. Each time the share makes a new high my stop loss moves upwards and I change my automatic stop to the new price level. I was doing this on a daily basis with the FMG trade.

By 14 May the share had risen 25 per cent in the five trading days since I opened the trade. Based on the share's ATR it had the potential to move 3.5 per cent of its share price in a day and it had moved beyond this average for five days.

I have a rule in my trading plan that if a share moves at a fast pace in a short space of time, I can consider selling half the trade or tightening the stop loss. It is a judgement call and it is sometimes difficult to know what to do when you are in this situation. I decided to sell half the trade to protect my windfall profits. I exited 250 CFDs on 14 May at $32.34 and held the remainder.

The share continued to rise even higher after I exited and reached $38.50 three days later. This was a total rise of 48 per cent since I entered the trade. I was thinking to myself: 'Wow—this is too good to be true—don't I wish I was still holding on to the entire trade!' But hindsight is a wonderful thing with trading and you can always see what would have been best after the event. From experience I have found that selling half has always made it easier for me to hold the remainder of the trade.

When I was a beginner trader, the temptation to take profits was so strong that it would overcome me and I would exit the entire trade. These days I only sell half when I am in a windfall profit position like this because there could be more profits to be had. In this case, there were.

Because the share had risen by nearly 50 per cent of its value in under two weeks, I decided to tighten my stop loss on the remaining trade. I was sold out on 21 May at $33.77 when the share hit my automatic stop loss during the day. I held this trade for a total of 14 days and made a profit of $3494.50, which equated to a return of 527 per cent on the capital I outlaid on the trade and a 27 per cent return on the total trade size (not taking margins into account).

Figure 24.4 shows how the trade progressed and my actual entry and exit points.

Figure 24.4: Fortescue Metals Group (daily chart)

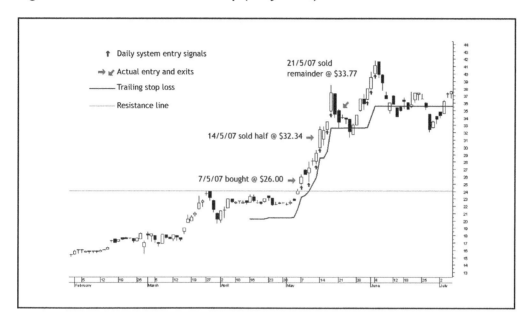

Trade 2: IINet Limited (IIN)

I decided to buy IIN on the same day as FMG because they both came up in my daily system scan and both matched my entry system rules.

This share had been trending sideways for the past three months and when it broke to new highs above its $1.50 resistance, my system gave me a buy signal and I bought 7000 CFDs at $1.59 on 7 May. I set the initial stop loss below resistance at $1.39 and used this to position size the trade. The margin on the trade was 10 per cent and the details of my entry are summarised below.

Entry date:	7 May 2007
Buy price:	$1.59
Initial stop loss:	$1.39
Risk:	$0.20
Risk value:	$1500.00
No. of shares:	7500
Actual purchased:	7000
Total trade size:	$11 130.00
Margin:	10%
Brokerage costs:	$11.13
Capital outlay on trade:	$1124.13

I managed the trade using my mechanical trailing stop loss and raised the stop as the share moved my way. The share started out slowly with some nice small rises and then had a large jump on 14 May, rising nearly 12 per cent of its share price in one day. IIN had an ATR of $0.07, so it had the potential to rise by approximately 4 per cent of its share price in one day. This means the rise on 14 May was three times its normal activity.

On the same day, FMG had a large rise and I decided to sell half of that trade (as detailed previously). I had a strong temptation to sell half IIN as well but assessed that it had risen a total of 19 per cent from my entry, whereas FMG had risen an impressive 25 per cent from my entry, so I made the call to hold the full position in IIN and sell half of FMG instead.

The next day the share fell with a strong black candle wiping out its gains from the previous day. My stop loss was not hit, so I remained in the trade. I was annoyed that I hadn't sold half IIN the previous day, but I was past the days of beating myself up inside my head and pushed those thoughts aside.

Figure 24.5 shows how the trade progressed and my entry and exit points.

Figure 24.5: IINet Limited (daily chart)

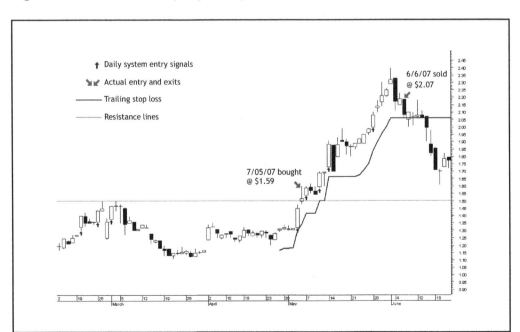

IIN did rise and make up for this fall the next trade day, then trended sideways for a few days while my stop stayed at the same price level. Eventually, IIN started to rise again and my stop loss also rose.

On 28 May, IIN broke through the $2.00 barrier and continued higher each day, reaching its final high on 1 June at $2.32. The competition was now over but I decided to remain in the trade. The share fell after this high and I was sold out of the trade at $2.07 when my automatic stop loss was hit on 6 June. I had held this trade for a total of 30 days and made a profit of $3334.38, which was a return of 298 per cent on my capital outlay and 30 per cent on the total trade size.

Trade 3: Queensland Gas Company (QGC)

QGC was my top winning trade after the competition ended. The share had been trending sideways and it appeared in my daily system scan on 15 May when it broke to new highs above its resistance level of $1.75. I bought QGC on this day at $1.79 and set my initial stop loss at $1.64. The margin on the trade was 10 per cent and the details of my entry are summarised below.

Entry date:	15 May 2007
Buy price:	$1.79
Initial stop loss:	$1.64
Risk:	$0.15
Risk value:	$1500.00
No. of shares:	10000
Actual purchased:	9500
Total trade size:	$17005.00
Margin:	10%
Brokerage costs:	$17.00
Capital outlay on trade:	$1717.50

As you can see, I could have bought 10000 CFDs, but I have a habit of rounding down the quantity to allow for brokerage costs. I bought 9500 instead.

The share continued to rise strongly after I opened it and moved easily above the next round number of $2.00 on 23 May. I always like it when shares rise above round numbers because these price levels can sometimes be difficult to break through. It is common for shares to pause and start to form resistance levels at round numbers.

Once again I was in the enjoyable position of moving my stop upwards on a daily basis as the share continued to rise. When the competition closed on 31 May it was trading at $2.31 and I continued to hold the trade and let my profits run. It had a phenomenal rise on 1 June, rising as high as $2.63 before settling back to close at $2.40. It was 17 days (or 13 trading days) since I had entered the trade and the share had risen by 34 per cent. Based on the share's ATR value at this time, it could rise approximately 3.3 per cent of its share price on a daily basis, so this was well within its capabilities and nothing to be alarmed about.

On 1 June, the share provided me with a pyramid signal to buy more after it rose past $2.43. I decided to wait and see if it could move past the next round number barrier of $2.50 and buy if it broke this price level. The share, however, settled down at this point and trended sideways for two weeks. My trailing stop loss stopped moving and remained at $2.26 from 5 June to 21 June. I pyramided and bought more once the share rose back above $2.50, sizing the trade with my current stop loss of $2.26 and halving my risk percentage. The details of my second entry into QGC are summarised below.

Entry date:	18 June 2007
Buy price:	$2.54
Initial stop loss:	$2.26
Risk:	$0.28
Risk value:	$750.00
No. of shares:	2678
Actual purchased:	2000
Total trade size:	$5080.00
Margin:	10%
Brokerage costs:	$10.00
Capital outlay on trade:	$518.00

My current trading capital was totaling $110 000 (based on $90 000 in the bank and approximately $20 000 in my CMC Markets trading account). This meant that no single trade should exceed $22 000 in total (20 per cent × 110 000). I toned back the position size and bought 2000 CFDs—keeping the total buy value of the two trades at $22 000.

The share took off again on 22 June, breaking above its short-term consolidation area and reaching new highs—which is what I was hoping would happen, especially since I had pyramided and added to the trade. It continued to rise and moved above the next round number of $3.00 on 4 July. By this time I was very excited—another round number had been passed and I now had a larger trade active with a pyramid position.

These are the trades that you know will make you the big money and they become your little babies that you keep a watchful eye on. All sorts of thoughts started to go through my head ('Can it keep on going up like this? It has to end soon!'). I just pushed these thoughts aside and was happy that I had found my next big winner.

On 5 July the share had another strong rise, hitting a high of $3.23. This was the last white candle that the share generated before I was stopped out of the trade. The next day, QGC peaked at $3.30 and then collapsed with a black engulfing candle falling past $3.00 and closing at $2.98. This was a strong reversal candlestick pattern and not something you like to see occurring in a trade. I tightened my stop loss to $2.88 and was automatically stopped out at this price level the next trading day on 9 July, after the weekend.

I held the trade for a total of 55 days and made a profit of $10 974. That was a return of 490 per cent on the total capital outlay of both trades (600 per cent on the initial trade from the competition), which equates to a return of 49 per cent on the total trade size (not considering margins). Figure 24.6 shows how the trade progressed and my entry and exit points.

Figure 24.6: Queensland Gas Company (daily chart)

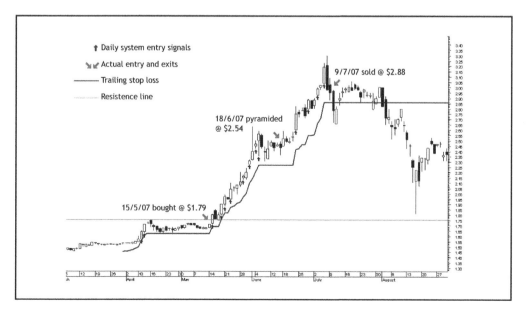

Trade 4: Tabcorp Holdings (TAH)

Tabcorp was my biggest losing trade of the competition and a good example with which to demonstrate exactly how I keep my losses small on the trades that fail.

The set-up was the same as all the other trades, but this one failed. The share had been trending sideways for over two years below a resistance level of $18.00 and finally broke to new highs above this level and provided me with a buy signal. It appeared in my MetaStock scan and met all my trading rules, so I bought 1000 CFDs on 4 May at $18.70, setting an initial stop loss at $17.36.

Entry date:	4 May 2007
Buy price:	$18.70
Initial stop loss:	$17.36
Risk:	$1.34
Risk value:	$1500.00
No. of shares:	1119
Actual purchased:	1000
Total trade size:	$18 700.00
Margin:	5%
Brokerage costs:	$18.70
Capital outlay on trade:	$953.70

Unfortunately, three days after I opened the trade, TAH collapsed back under its $18.00 resistance level. This is not something that you like to see happen. Technically, you want the share to hold its resistance and see this level become support for the new price activity. This did not occur with this share and it failed to remain above this level.

I was tempted to exit this trade at this stage, but I decided to follow my stop loss and give the trade more time to see if it would rise again above its resistance level. This was not to be and I was automatically exited out of the trade at my initial stop loss of $17.36 on 16 May. TAH never managed to rise back above $18.00, even after I was taken out of the trade. This is a good example of a failed technical signal.

I held the trade for a total of 12 days and my return was −144 per cent on the capital I outlaid to open the trade, and −7 per cent on the total trade size.

As I have discussed previously in this book, there is no magic indicator and no trading signal is 100 per cent accurate. Money management is the only control you have in the market and this trade shows how I followed my trading rules and exited this trade at my initial stop loss, ensuring that the loss was kept small. TAH never recovered and at the time of writing this book it was trading at $11.00. By exiting the trade at a small loss I was able to free up my capital from a poorly performing trade and put the money into another trade and have it work hard for me. As it happened, QGC came along and I entered this on 15 May, one day before I was exited out of TAH.

Figure 24.7 shows how the trade progressed and my entry and exit points.

Figure 24.7: Tabcorp Holdings (daily chart)

As my results in this chapter show, all the entries were similar and they were all taken when they appeared in my daily trading system. Not every share performed the same way and not every trade will. That is why risk management is so important and is the only tool that will ensure your survival in the markets.

If you are interested in seeing more details of all my trades from the competition I have an audio recording from a teleconference I ran on the event and copies of all the charts available for purchase at <www.smarttrading.com.au>.

25

Conclusion

Trading is tough. It's not easy when you first start out and it will be a challenge — there is no doubt about that. It is like starting your first job — you have no idea of what you are doing at first and it takes time and effort to learn the ropes and get into a routine. You will spend a lot more time in the early days developing your new skills and completing your personal trading plan, but once you have finalised your plan and built confidence with your trading system, you will have much more time to concentrate on your trading.

My goal in writing this book has been to guide you and point you in the right direction to complete your own personal trading plan. Your plan will be individual — your trading style, amount of capital, risk exposure, reasons for trading and personality are all unique and you need to develop a plan that reflects this.

If you have already done the hard work and finished your plan — congratulations! It is a big task and you deserve a pat on the back. It is now time to put your plan into action and start investing your money in the market — this will be when the real learning starts. Remember to start small and add more money as you gain confidence. There is no hurry — as I've said before, the market is open five days a week for your entire life, so don't rush it.

If you have begun developing your plan, you have made a positive start and you need to focus on completing it. You may have some gaps to fill in and you may want to spend some time educating yourself further, researching different trading systems and styles to find one that suits you. Remember that there is no Holy Grail, there is no magic indicator and there is no 100 per cent winning trading system. People can spend years searching for the right system yet still end up exactly where they started, so don't get hung up looking for the perfect system. Find one that suits your style of trading and get started.

If you haven't put in the hard work and written your trading plan yet, go back and re-read the relevant sections of this book and download your free *Smart Trading Plan Template* from <www.smarttrading.com.au> and get started.

Becoming a consistently profitable trader requires time and discipline. You must make the effort to complete your trading plan and follow it carefully once it is finished. The market rewards traders who put in the effort to complete their personal trading plans and have the discipline to follow them.

Your development as a trader will be an ongoing journey of self-discovery and growth. To ensure you stay focused and don't lose sight of the big picture, make a habit of regularly reviewing your trading plan and your goals and objectives. It may change over time as you develop as a trader and you need to update it as you evolve and progress.

As I said at the beginning of the book, your trading plan is your road map in the market — without it you will get lost.

I wish you well in your trading journey.

Appendix A: the trading plan

The trading plan example statements (from the end of each chapter) are collated here to show you how a trading plan might look in its entirety.

Goals and objectives

Why am I trading?

I am trading as a means to increase my net worth. It puts me in control of my wealth creation and offers me the opportunity to live a comfortable lifestyle. It is something that I am passionate about and I am prepared to put in as much time and dedication as is required to succeed.

Goals

My goals as a trader are to:

- become the best trader I can possibly be

- push myself forward and acquire the essential skills and psychological stability to conquer the trading game; this will involve taking occasional losses and having to confront my fears

- use technical analysis to assist me in my trading decisions and develop a long-term trend-following trading system

- manage my risk and protect my capital with the long-term goal of being consistently profitable

- to give back and support the community; as my trading profits increase, I plan to donate a percentage of my profits to a chosen charity each year.

Trading edge

I believe my edge in the market is my trading strategy and personality. My trading strategy focuses on long-term trends and using money management strategies to protect my capital and let my profits run. It will be my determination, focus, motivation and organisation that will ensure I stay focused on my goals and aim for success in the markets.

Trading returns and objectives

I will trade the Australian stock market through shares and aim to achieve the following:

Year	Goal
One	To survive
Two	To generate a higher rate of return than a term deposit rate
Three (and beyond)	To outperform the All Ordinaries each and every year

Trading structure

At first, I will trade in my individual name. Once my account size and profits increase, I will seek the advice of an accountant to set up an alternative structure that suits my new requirements.

Trading tools

- I will use MetaStock software to view charts and scan the market for trading opportunities. The stock market data will be provided by DataHQ <www.smarttradingdata.com.au>.

- Microsoft software, such as Excel and Word, will be used for gathering trading notes. I will use the Smart Trader Spreadsheet for tracking and managing my trades <www.smarttrading.com.au>.

- A range of websites will be used to view share price and market action:

  » My broker's website will be used to view market depth, trade shares and review upcoming dividends.

  » The Trading Room website <www.tradingroom.com.au> will be used as a backup to view share price information and market news.

  » The ASX website <www.asx.com.au> will be a source of information on the Australian stock market.

  » The *Australian Financial Review* <www.afr.com.au> will be a source of market news and financial information.

  » Yahoo finance <www.yahoo.com.au/finance> will be another source for market news and financial information.

- Other websites of interest:

  » Nasdaq <www.nasdaq.com> will be used to view the US stock market performance.

  » Stock Charts <www.stockcharts.com> will enable me to view technical charts of US stocks and indices.

  » Kitco <www.kitco.com> will be a source of information and charts of gold and other precious metals.

- I have selected _____ as my broker for trading shares.

- I will use a mobile phone to manage my portfolio through SMS and wireless internet, especially when I am travelling.

- I will build up a library of educational books on trading that are recommended by authors and other traders I know. I will regularly attend courses to educate myself on the business of trading.

Trading style

I will focus on long-term investing in the Australian stock market. I am a trend follower and my plan is to seek out rising shares, build a profitable portfolio and gain additional income through dividends. I will use technical analysis and let the charts tell me when the trend is over and it is time to exit.

Trading instruments

I have chosen to trade the Australian market only and focus on the S&P/ASX 300 shares to ensure sufficient liquidity and price discovery.

Indicators

To measure	Selected indicator
The trend	Trendlines, support/resistance lines, 30-week exponential moving average
Momentum	MACD histogram
Volatility	Average true range (ATR)
Market strength	Volume

Money management

Initially, I will allocate myself a trading account of $50 000 to trade up to a total of six positions. I will:

- allocate this capital to S&P/ASX 300 stocks only

- position size my trades based on 2 per cent risk ($1000)

- ensure no single position exceeds 25 per cent ($12 500)

- manage a portfolio heat level of 6 per cent.

Once I have gained enough confidence with my trading I will add another $50 000 to my trading account and then reassess my risk levels.

Market exposure

During a cluster of losses I will take some time out and reassess things. I will re-enter the market when I feel ready by halving my position size and increase it when I am confident enough to do so.

I will also lessen my exposure in the market when I go away on holidays or if I can't focus on trading during difficult times in my life.

I am a long-term trader and will only trade long in the market. During bear markets I will follow my stop-loss strategy and exit trades as my stops are hit. I will sit out of the market until I see it becoming healthy again and then I will re-enter and slowly build positions back into the market.

The trading system

Objective:

Build a long-term portfolio of shares by searching the market for shares in an existing uptrend and stay with this long-term trend until signs appear that the trend is changing.

Market selection:

S&P/ASX 300 stocks only.

Market direction:

Long only.

The entry

Ideal set-up criteria:

Share is healthy and the chart shows:

- it is in an uptrend with no immediate overhead resistance

- it is trending above its long-term moving average

- it has a rising momentum indicator

- there is increasing volume supporting the trend.

Trigger for entry:

Share is breaking through to new highs or retracing and bouncing off its trendline.

Placing the order:

I will place my orders 'at market' after the market has settled.

Trade management strategy

Stop losses:

- The initial stop loss will be set either below the trendline or below a significant support level.

- Once the trade is in profit by the initial risk the stop loss will be moved to a breakeven stop—which is the buy price.

- The trendline will then be used as the trailing profit stop and I will exit if this breaks anytime.

- A time stop will be set for a three-month period. This means if my stop loss has not moved to a breakeven stop within three months I will consider exiting.

- If at any stage the share becomes volatile and starts rising a large amount in a short space of time, I will sell half and take windfall profits.

- I will set automatic stop losses in the market and change these as required, so I will be automatically exited out of the trade when the share hits my stop.

Pyramiding

Once my stop loss has moved to a trailing profit stop, I will keep my eye on the share and consider purchasing more if another entry trigger is provided. I will size the trade based on half the risk of the initial position. The new trade will then be managed the same as the initial position.

Trading routine

Daily routine

- If my weekly routine confirms I can open a new trade, I will review my watchlist folder and open a trade if a trigger presents itself.

Weekly routine

- Review the charts of my current open trades and determine whether any action should be taken, such as moving stop losses or adding more shares to a profitable trade.

- Update my Smart Trader Spreadsheet with any changes to my portfolio and check my current available capital and portfolio heat to see if I can open any new positions.

- Scan the market for long-term trading opportunities and add any shares that match my trading rules to my watchlist.

Monthly routine

- Review the charts of the world market indices and All Ords to determine the overall health and trend of the world markets.

- Review the charts of the major Australian sector indices to determine the overall health and trend of these sectors.

- Back up my computer.

Quarterly routine

- Read one book on the markets or enroll in a trading course to expand my trading knowledge and improve my skills.

Annual routine

- Review my yearly trading performance and total return on investment compared to the All Ords financial year performance. Did I meet my trading goals for the year? Do I need to make any changes to my trading strategy?

- Review my trading plan to remind myself of my goals and update it with any changes I have made to my trading strategy.

- With the assistance of an accountant, complete and submit my annual tax return.

Trade evaluation

I will make a regular habit of reviewing each trade as I close it out to determine if I am developing any bad habits in the market.

I will use the *Smart Trader Spreadsheet* to track and manage all my trading activity in the market and assess my profitability and review my trading performance on a yearly basis.

If my statistics and trade analysis show that things are going wrong I will take a step back from my trading and reassess myself and my trading systems.

Contingency plan

As part of my monthly routine I will regularly make backups of my computer files and store them in a separate location.

I have equipment in place to protect me if there is a power surge or power outage and a dial-up internet connection as backup in case broadband connection problems occur. I will keep my broker's phone number handy so that I can call to make any changes to my portfolio during these times.

I know that no matter what happens, my stop losses rule and will tell me when to exit. By managing my maximum open market risk through portfolio heat I will never be overexposed in the marketplace and will be aware of my worst-case scenario at all times.

Personal rules

For your personal completion.

Appendix B: resources

Websites

\<www.smarttrading.com.au\>	The Smart Trading website—download your *Free Book Bonuses* and check out Justine's range of products and training packages
\<www.afr.com.au\>	Australian Financial Review website
\<www.asx.com.au\>	Official website of the Australian Securites Exchange
\<www.equis.com\>	Official MetaStock technical analysis software website
\<www.incrediblecharts.com\>	Free charting software for Australian charts and indices
\<www.kitco.com\>	Information and charts for gold and other precious metals
\<www.nasdaq.com\>	US stock market index updates, market news, quotes and information
\<www.smarttrading.com.au/books\>	Moneybags website—provides trading books and other products for purchase and delivery to your door
\<www.smarttradingdata.com.au\>	DataHQ website—provides market data for the ASX, SGX and US exchanges for MetaStock

<www.stockcharts.com>	US stock charts and indices
<www.tradingroom.com.au>	Australian stock market news, quotes and information
<www.yahoo.com.au/finance>	Australian stock market news, charts and financial market information
<www.yte.com.au>	Bi-monthly magazine for traders and investors in CFDs, stocks, options, futures, forex and commodities

Reading material

Bedford, Louise, *The Secret of Candlestick Charting*, Wrightbooks, 2000

Bedford, Louise, *Trading Secrets*, Wrightbooks, 2001

Darvas, Nicolas, *How I made $2,000,000 in the Stock Market*, Lyle Stuart Inc., 1986

Diaz, Eva, *Real Traders, Real Lives, Real Money*, Wrightbooks, 2006

Diaz, Eva, *Real Traders II*, Wrightbooks, 2007

Douglas, Mark, *Trading in the Zone*, Prentice Hall, 2000

Elder, Dr Alexander, *Trading for a Living*, John Wiley & Sons, 1993

Pollard, Justine, *Smart Technical Analysis Home Study Course*, © Smart Trading Pty Ltd, 2002

Schwager, Jack D, *Market Wizards: Interviews with Top Traders*, NYIF Corp, 1989

Stanton, Dr Harry E, *Let the Trade Wins Flow: Psychology for Super Traders*, © Dr H.E. Stanton, 1997

Tate, Chris, *Taming the Bear*, Wrightbooks, 1999

Tate, Chris, *The Art of Trading* (2nd ed.), Wrightbooks, 2001

Tharp, Dr Van K , *Trade Your Way to Financial Freedom*, McGraw-Hill, 1999

Weinstein, Stan, *Secrets for Profiting in Bull and Bear Markets*, McGraw-Hill, 1988

Glossary

All Ordinaries index   a share price index that measures the market price of the major stocks listed on the Australian Securities Exchange

ask (asking price)   the price a seller wants for the sale of his or her shares (also referred to as the seller's price)

average hold time   the average time that you hold a trade open for, calculated by adding the number of days that you have held every trade and dividing that figure by the total number of trades

average loss size   calculated by adding up all the losses on your losing trades and dividing this by the total number of losing trades

average true range (ATR)   a volatility indicator that tells you the average price movement of a particular share in one day or over a set period of time

average win size   calculated by adding up all the profits on your winning trades and dividing this by the total number of winning trades

back test	a method of testing a trading system's performance by applying it to historical data
bar chart	a chart that is made up of a series of price bars, or vertical bars, that represent the price activity for the share over a set period
bearish	a share is described as bearish if it is in a downtrend
bear market	a market where share prices are generally falling
bid	also referred to as the buyer's price, it is the price a buyer is willing to pay to purchase a share
black box	software that is pre-coded with a set system that provides buy and sell signals
black candle	when a share price closes lower than it opened, it is displayed as a black candle
blue chip	established companies that tend to offer a good dividend yield
breakeven stop	a stop loss set at the price level at which you bought the stock (give or take brokerage costs), so you can lock in a no-loss trade
breakout	when the share price moves out (or breaks out) of a trading range or consolidation area
brokerage	commissions charged by a broker
bullish	a share is described as bullish if it is in an uptrend
bull market	a market where share prices are generally increasing

call option/warrant	gives the buyer the right (but not the obligation) to buy a share at a set price on or before a set expiry date
candlestick chart	a charting technique that connects the open and the close prices with a white or black rectangle (candle body), and the highest and lowest price for the share appear as wicks from the candle's body
capital	the amount of money or equity that you have to devote to trading
capitalisation	see *market capitalisation*
commodities	assets (usually agricultural products or metals) that are traded on the commodity markets such as the Sydney Futures Exchange or via CFDs
consolidation	see *sideways trend*
contract for difference (CFD)	an agreement or contract between two parties (usually you and your CFD provider) that offers the benefits of trading shares without physically owning them
day trader	a trader who opens and closes his or her trades within the same day
delisted	shares that are removed from the stock exchange and can no longer be traded
derivatives	financial instruments derived from an underlying asset, such as options, warrants, CFDs and futures
divergence	occurs when the share price moves in the opposite direction to an indicator
dividend	distribution of a company's profits to its shareholders

dividend yield	annual percentage return that shareholders receive in the form of dividends from the company, calculated by dividing the total dividends of the last 12 months by the company's share price
double top	a top reversal pattern that occurs when a share makes two equal highs forming two peaks (like an M shape)
downtrend	prices move downwards, making a series of lower highs and lower lows (also referred to as bearish trends or bear markets)
downtrend line	a downward-sloping diagonal line connecting the price highs from left to right
drawdown	the amount of money lost due to one or more losing trades
earnings per share (EPS)	the figure provided by a company in its annual reporting, produced by dividing the company's net annual profit after tax by the number of shares on issue, producing a cents per share result
equal portions	a position-sizing method that involves dividing your trading capital into a certain number of equal amounts and then purchasing shares based on these amounts
equities	another term for *shares*
equity curve	a graphical representation of changes in your trading account balance
ex-dividend date	also referred to as the ex-date, every person who owns the share on this day will be entitled to receive the dividend—the share will reduce in price to compensate for this

foreign exchange (FX)	the trading of foreign currencies (such as the Australian dollar against the US dollar) through the Futures Exchange or through CFDs
franking credits	some companies pay company tax on dividends before distributing them to shareholders, who then receive franking credits which they claim in their tax return to ensure they do not pay tax on them twice
fundamental analysis	an analysis based on the use of economic data and company statistics to forecast prices
futures	contracts to buy and sell specified commodities or financial instruments at a specified date in the future, traded in Australia on the Sydney Futures Exchange
Global Industry Classification Standard (GICS)	a standardised classification system that classifies ASX-listed shares into 12 industry groups (or sectors)
grey box	a charting package that provides some freedom to create your own stock scans, but limits you to a set of parameters
guaranteed stop loss order (GSLO)	stop-loss orders that are guaranteed at a set price, only available for a fee through some CFD providers
hedge	a method of protecting your portfolio through the use of put options/warrants or other instruments
illiquid	instruments that lack demand and have only a few buyers or sellers available, making them difficult to buy or sell at the price you want

index

a measure of a change in value of a group of securities based on market capitalisation (for example, the All Ordinaries index)

indicator

a calculation of a set of criteria that can be used to measure something specific, such as volatility, momentum and market strength

industry sector

see *Global Industry Classification Standard*

initial stop loss

the first stop you set before opening a trade with the aim of limiting your losses and preserving your capital

instrument

an asset or contract that has a monetary value that can be traded between two parties

intraday

price movements of an instrument within a trading day

leverage

exposure to an instrument at a fraction of the normal price, usually through the use of margin or derivative instruments

limit order

an order to buy or sell a share at a set price limit

line chart

a chart made up of a single line that is plotted based on the closing price of the share or index

liquidity

instruments with strong demand that have a significant number of buyers and sellers available, making it easy to buy and sell

long

when you own a share, you have a long position in that security—your view on the share is usually bullish and you buy it with the goal of selling at a higher price in the future

long-term trading a style of trading usually referred to as 'buy and hold', suited to investors who want to retain a share for a long period of time to receive an income from dividends and enjoy the benefit of large capital gains

MACD (moving average convergence divergence) a trend-following indicator that provides signals based on a calculation of a series of moving averages—it appears on a chart as a solid line and a dashed line

MACD histogram a momentum indicator that is produced from the MACD indicator, calculated by taking the difference between the two MACD lines and plotting this to form a histogram that oscillates above and below a zero line into positive and negative territory

margin a deposit required from a broker to open a position—margin is usually required when trading CFDs, writing options or short selling shares

market capitalisation determines which indices a share belongs to—calculated by multiplying the share price by the total number of shares on issue

market depth the queue of buyers and sellers who have placed bids and offers in the market for the share

market order when you place an order to buy a share at the current available market price, which is the current offer price from the next available seller (these orders can only be placed during market hours and when the share is trading)

maximum position size the maximum size, based on a set percentage of your capital, that you will take out on any one trade to ensure you diversify your capital in the market

medium-term trading	holding a trade anywhere from a few weeks to a few months
momentum	measures the speed at which prices move over a set period of time
moving average	plotted on a chart to form a smoothed line of the share price, by taking the sum of the closing prices and averaging them out over a set period
open interest	the total number of outstanding contracts on a specific underlying security, comparable to volume
open market risk	your financial position if all your trades were to hit their stop losses in one day
options	a derivative instrument that grants the right (but not the obligation) to buy or sell a share at a set price, on or before the expiry date
percentage risk	the percentage of your capital that you are prepared to lose on any one trade
period	an amount of time that you select for a chart (such as daily, weekly or monthly) or for an indicator (such as a 30-day moving average)
portfolio heat	a technique that professional traders use to manage and quantify their total open market risk (see *open market risk*)
position	established when you enter a trade of any sort in the markets (long or short)
position sizing	a method used to determine how many shares you can buy based on your personal risk profile and the amount of capital you have available

price/earnings ratio (P/E ratio)	calculated by dividing the current share price by its earnings per share (EPS) over the last 12 months
profit stop	a profit target stop—you exit the trade once it achieves this level
psychological stop	exiting your positions in the market due to psychological reasons brought on by events such as travelling, feeling ill or moving house
pullback	see *retracement*
put option/warrant	puts allow you to profit from share price falls by giving the buyer the right, but not the obligation, to sell the share at a set price on or before a set expiry date
pyramiding	progressively adding to a profitable position— usually the initial trade is the largest and then you add smaller parcels as the share continues your way
reliability	the number of winning trades divided by your total number of trades, compared with your number of losing trades divided by your total number of trades
resistance	the price level to which the price consistently rises and then falls away from, acting as a ceiling to the share price activity
retracement	the share moves back to its trendline and bounces (also known as a correction)
sector	a group of shares that have common characteristics—sectors include healthcare, telecommunications, finance and energy (see also *GICS*)

securities	another term for *shares*
set-up	the conditions that must be present before you would consider adding an instrument to your watchlist
shares	also referred to as stocks, securities and equities—a share is a small portion of a company that you can buy either privately or through a listed company on the stock market
short selling	your view on a share is usually bearish—you borrow shares and sell them with an obligation to return the shares in the future when they are bought back (shorting can also be undertaken with derivative instruments such as put options/warrants or CFDs)
short-term trading	holding a trade anywhere from a few minutes to a few days
sideways trend	occurs when the share is consolidating and is not making higher highs or lower lows; it is trending sideways between a support and a resistance level
slippage	the difference between the expected stop-loss price and the actual price at which you exit
spread	the difference between the bid and asking price of the buyers and sellers in the market
stop loss	a predetermined price at which a trader will exit a position in order to protect his or her capital
support	the price level to which the share price consistently falls and then bounces off and moves higher, acting as a floor to the share price activity

technical analysis	involves reviewing actual price and volume activity of a share using charts to determine if it is healthy or unhealthy
time stop	a limit on the length of time you will stay in a trade if the share does not move as expected
tool box	a charting package that gives you the freedom to code it as you desire and create your own personal stock market scans and indicators
trading plan	your personal business plan that sets out how you will trade the markets
trading range	see *sideways trend*
trading system	this includes your entry rules (set-up and triggers) and exit rules. It might be a mechanical system that you have coded into a charting package to scan the market for you, or it may be a manual system whereby you look at charts or research companies that meet your trading system criteria
trailing profit stop	moving a stop in the direction of the trend in order to protect your open profits as a trade moves favourably your way
trend	see *uptrend, downtrend* and *sideways trend*
trendline	significant reference lines that are drawn diagonally, connecting either the price highs or lows on a chart
trigger	the criteria that prompts you to open a trade in the market
uptrend	prices move upwards making a series of higher highs and higher lows, also referred to as bullish trends or bull markets

uptrend line	drawn on the chart by joining the price lows with an upward sloping diagonal line, connecting the lows from left to right
volatility	measures the fluctuation in prices (either up or down) over a set period of time
volume	the total number of shares that change hands each trade day, usually plotted as a histogram at the bottom of a share chart
warrant	a derivative instrument issued by financial institutions—available in the form of calls and puts, warrants grant you the right (but not the obligation) to buy or sell a share at a set price, on or before the expiry date
white candle	if a share rises, closing higher in price than it opened, it will be displayed as a white candle
win to loss size ratio	calculated by dividing your average win size by your average loss size

Index

Discover the SMARTER way to trade

Learning to master trading can be very challenging and Smart Trading is dedicated to assisting you to become a Smarter Trader. From home study courses to personal mentoring, you will learn directly from Justine Pollard, a professional trader who specialises in:

- technical analysis trading (charting)

- mechanical trading system design

- money and risk-management strategies

- CFD and share trading

- personal trading plan development

- trade management (including spreadsheet software)

- using MetaStock software.

It is never too late to learn and the cost of education is a small price to pay compared to the cost of trading losses and mistakes. For more information visit:

<www.smarttrading.com.au>

More opportunities to learn from Justine Pollard

Justine has produced a range of trading courses and products — visit
<www.smarttrading.com.au> for more information on these and many more products:

Smart Technical Analysis Home Study Course

This course will teach you the skill of technical analysis and
understanding how to read the health of a share through
viewing charts. The course includes lots of exercises to
put your knowledge into practice and develop your own
personal set of trading rules for entries and exits.

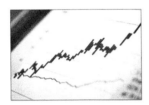

Smart Trading Plan & System Development Online Course

This is the ultimate online audio course that will take your
technical analysis knowledge to the next level and assist
you in completing your own personal trading plan. You
will discover exactly how Justine trades the markets — her
actual entry, exit and money management strategies.

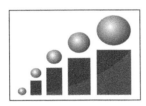

Smart Traders Mastermind

Exclusive client membership program which includes
continued support and mentoring through quarterly
teleconference calls with Justine and a private discussion
forum. It's an opportunity to connect with a group of like-
minded traders and continue to develop your trading skills.

Smart Trader Spreadsheet

This spreadsheet, specifically designed and used by Justine,
will assist you in tracking and recording all your trades,
manage your business of trading and risk exposure, and
provide you with performance measurement tools to
monitor and evaluate your performance in the market at
any point in time.

Don't waste time — visit <www.smarttrading.com.au> and register for your free
trading tips and start discovering the SMARTER way to trade.

Printed and bound by CPI Group (UK) Ltd, Croydon, CR0 4YY

06/01/2025

14620904-0001